The Academy of Golf
at PGA National

PLAY BETTER

GOLF

FOR WOMEN

Foreword by
Laura Davies

THIS IS A CARLTON BOOK

This edition published in 1997

10 9 8 7 6 5 4 3 2 1

Text © Mike Adams, T.J. Tomasi and Kathryn Maloney
Design and diagrams copyright © Carlton Books
Limited 1997

A CIP catalogue record for this book is available from
the British Library.

ISBN 1 85868 248 7

Project Editors: Martin Corteel/Julian Flanders
Production: Garry Lewis
Editor: Heather Thomas
Designer: Al Rockall

Printed and Bound in Dubai

Note: For convenience of presentation, we have
presented the material in this book for right-handed
golfers. Obviously, the mechanics of the golf swing
will apply to all golfers.

Picture Credits
Jeff Ackerly: pages 10, 14, 15 (top), 43, 44, 45, 114,
115, 116, 119, 121, 134, 135, 136 (side bar), 137,
141, and 153; Allsport/David Cannon page 3 (left),
Allsport/Andrew Redington page 3 (centre),
Allsport/J.D. Cuban page 5; Arizona State University:
page 122; Fazio Design: page 143; Marc Feldman:
pages 17 (left), 20, 32, 50, 53, 55, 56, 57, 59, 61, 63,
65, 67, 71, 88, 89, 94, 99 and 100; Henry-Griffiths:
pages 11, 15 (bottom), 17 (right); Ironhorse Country
Club: page 154; Kathryn Maloney: pages 8, 16, 19,
21, 127 (top), 131, 149, 150 and 151; Ken
May: pages 128 and 138; J. Miller: page 142; Mark
Newcombe page 3 (right); PGA National Resort:
pages 6, 117, 120, 124, 127 (bottom), 136, 140, 144,
145, 146, 147, 152 and 155; Warren Raatz: pages 49,
78, 79, 91, 92, 93, 104, 106, 107, 109, 111, 112, 113
and 118; Terry Renna: pages 22, 23, 24, 25, 26, 27,
28, 29, 30, 31, 33, 34, 35, 36, 37, 38, 39, 40, 41, 42,
46, 47, 72, 73, 74, 75, 76, 77, 80, 82, 85, 86, 87, 96,
97, 98, 101 and 103; Titleist: page 12.

The Academy of Golf
at PGA National

PLAY BETTER
GOLF
FOR WOMEN

MIKE ADAMS, T.J. TOMASI AND
KATHRYN MALONEY

CARLTON

Contents

Foreword

By Laura Davies

Y ou may well ask why I have been chosen to write the foreword for *PGA National Play Better Golf for Women*. I have never made an in-depth study of technique, nor have I ever gone out of my way to get involved in conversations concerning the mechanics of the game. My method, as I have said in my own books, is to play by imitation. I watch great golfers such as Bernhard Langer, Seve Ballesteros and Freddie Couples and I play their swings over and over in my head almost as I would a song. Then, when I go to the practice ground, I endeavour to copy the shots I have seen.

That, as I say, is what has worked for me. However, I know of plenty of others who positively thrive on a deep-seated knowledge of what they are trying to do. Nick Faldo, for one. Who can argue with the way he goes about his business? Again, a number of my great friends in the world of women's golf are scarcely less analytical. Alison Nicholas and Trish Johnson are just two who spring to mind.

In looking through these pages, I must admit that there is plenty with which I can identify. For example, I particularly agree with what has been written on the subject of the follow-through. Namely, that the golfer should understand that a well-balanced finish is more than just that. If the finish is right, the chances are that the shot will have been a good one.

Very definitely, there are plenty of gems for the golfer looking to broaden her knowledge, but I would warn against the student in question becoming too enmeshed in technique.

Working things out on the practice ground is one thing but, when it gets to the course, everyone should endeavour to follow in the footsteps of Lady Heathcoat-Amory who, as Joyce Wethered, won five English championships in a row in the 1920s.

"On the practice ground," said Lady Amory, "I would do everything I could to ensure that my game was as technically correct as possible. Then, just before going out to play, I would cast all thoughts and theories out of my mind."

In other words, uninhibited shot-making has to be the ultimate aim, particularly for women golfers. Too many are either too self-conscious or too diffident to give the ball a healthy slosh.

Women are fast becoming a major factor in golf as they seek not only the joy and fun of the game, but also the competition, exercise, and benefits of combining business and golf.

In the United States, for example, research by the National Golf Foundation shows that there were 5.3 million women golfers as of 1996. In addition, 1.6 million people took up the game in 1994 and 34 percent of those were women. The Executive Women's Golf League, an organization dedicated to advancing women's participation in golf, was founded in 1991 with 28 members. Its growth has been exponential as this powerful organization of 88 chapters reached 14,000 members by the middle of 1996. The EWGL projected that there would be 18,000 women members by the end of 1996.

These statistics are a bright sign for the world

Golf is a game that offers a multitude of benefits, one of the greatest being the beauty of its playing field. The time for women to participate fully in this sport is long overdue.

of women's golf. There is strength in numbers and as the population of women golfers increases, so does their influence in the golf community. And in a sport that has so much to offer, the time for women to fully participate is long overdue.

The disappointing news though is that one out of every two women gives up golf after about two years. A survey done by the National Golf Foundation revealed that the majority of women listed playing better and knowing the "ins and outs" of golf as major factors that would encourage them to play more and stay in the game. This book is dedicated to giving you, the women of golf, a comprehensive guide to your golf swing and the many other facets of the game. Our goal is to help you enjoy "the game of a lifetime" for the rest of your life.

The problems

Much of the instruction women have received in the past was based on theories and methods developed with a man's body as the prototype. The physical differences between men and women are a detriment to women's golfing success only because these differences are largely ignored. Generally, the average woman has more flexibility, less muscular strength, especially in the upper body, and, because she is shaped differently than a man, a different center of balance. Ten years ago female golf instructors were few and only a handful of male golf instructors were willing to develop a teaching model that takes into consideration the student's individual differences.

In addition to poor instruction, women were held back in their effort to hit the ball better, because of the equipment they used. When women took up golf they often inherited men's clubs. In most cases these clubs were too long and too heavy for them. The common but incorrect solution was to simply cut a few inches off the shaft. This procedure actually stiffens the shaft and destroys the balance making these clubs even more unsuitable for women, especially a beginner.

Another contributing problem is the fact that golf courses are customarily designed for male golfers and the older the golf course, the more likely it is that the women's tees and other design features make the game more difficult. In many instances, the "forward" tees are only a few yards ahead of the men's tees, an insignificant yardage adjustment that served to aggravate a basic problem of women golfers—lack of distance. Often there are intimidating forced carries over hazards created by thoughtless design and, in some cases, the courses are almost unplayable for beginners. No wonder so many women golfers drop out.

As you will see in the chapter on course design, things have changed for the better although there are still remnants of inequality. Newer courses provide women's tees with distance adjustments but sometimes they are an afterthought to course design, and are often placed "off to the side" creating course management and strategy problems.

Although it's changing, some women initially have difficulty with golf due to their lack of opportunity to participate in other sports while growing up. Whereas golf skills can be learned at a rapid rate, sticking with the game through an uncomfortable initiation can make or break a golf career.

Finally, women are often intimidated by the nuances of a sport that has been dominated by men for centuries. To the uninitiated, golf is a complicated game both athletically and strategically, and its complexity is compounded by the unwritten rules of decorum both on the course and around the club house.

The solutions

This book offers a comprehensive program specifically tailored to you, the female golfer, with information regarding equipment, instruction, playing strategy, golf course architecture, golf

7

Golf's social benefits can enrich your personal life and your business contacts as well.

fitness guidelines, country club customs and insights from some of the leaders in the world of women's golf. Armed with a proper blueprint for playing better golf, you can begin to realize your potential as a golfer and enjoy the game fully.

First, whether your budget is large or small, you'll learn how to select the appropriate equipment to maximize your current golf skills. The instruction on the full swing and the short game will be for you specifically, with women as your role models.

If you have a daughter interested in golf, player profiles and advice from top collegiate coaches will outline how a championship golfer evolves. In addition, a program for golf fitness and golf-related strength training will help you enhance your abilities. If you're a beginner, you'll learn how to set appropriate goals and find advice for making those early rounds of golf enjoyable.

You'll also hear from top architects about how they have designed their newest courses and how they expect you to meet the challenge of their design from the forward tees. And, finally, the intricate customs and procedures of the golf world will be laid out in detail.

The authors

Mike Adams, a former PGA touring professional, is Director of the PGA's National Academy of Golf at Palm Beach Gardens, Florida. Known throughout the world as the "Swing Doctor," Adams has a keen eye for detecting swing flaws, and an impressive track record for correcting them. He is one of America's most sought-after golf teachers, teaching more than 3,000 individual lessons each year. Hollywood celebrities who have Adams to thank for their golf skills include Jack Nicholson, Michael Douglas, Willie Nelson and Tom Landry. President Bill Clinton worked with the "Swing Doctor" when he visited the PGA National in March 1995, and former President Gerald Ford was another pupil of Mike Adams. Recently voted one of America's 100 Best Golf Teachers by *Golf Magazine,* Adams writes instruction articles for *Golf Magazine, Golf Digest,* and *Golfing.*

Dr. T.J. Tomasi, a PGA Teaching Professional, is the Director of the Players School at the Academy of Golf at PGA National and, with over 20 years of experience, has taught all levels of players from beginners to experts. Dr. Tomasi was formerly the Director of Instruction at Chuck Hogan Golf Schools, and his innovative ideas and wealth of experience make him one of the most widely published golf professionals in the world. He has served as the chief instructional editor for *Golf Illustrated* and *Golfing Magazine,* as well as a contributing editor to publications such as *Golf Tips, Golf Magazine, Senior Golfer,* and *Inside Golf.* Dr. Tomasi's skills as a teacher are enhanced by his Ph.D. in Education that focused on Learning Theory. Ever the student, he continues his quest for knowledge of how students learn and the biomechanics of the golf swing.

Kathryn Maloney is an LPGA Teaching Professional at Ironhorse Country Club in West Palm Beach, Florida, and a contributing editor at *Golf Pro Magazine* where she writes a monthly column called Trends in Teaching based on interviews with leading teaching professionals. Formerly an Instructor at the Academy of Golf at PGA National and project manager for the book *PGA National Play Better Golf,* Kathryn also writes for leading US golf publications, such as *Golf Tips, Senior Golfer,* and *Golf for Women Magazine.*

Chapter one

Equipment

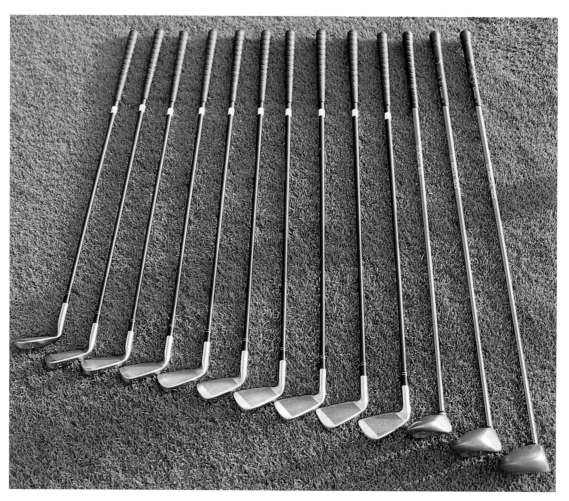

W hether you're just beginning your golf career or you're a seasoned player, it's important that your equipment is well suited to your body, your swing and your playing style. In the past when women took up the game they often used hand-me-down clubs from their husbands or friends. And since a woman's build, strength level and swing speed is usually different from that of a man, these "free" clubs actually cost a woman plenty in terms of her golf swing. Clubs inherited from men are often too heavy, as well as too long and stiff for many women. These clubs become a catalyst for swing errors that become

When choosing a set of golf clubs, you must be sure to have them tailored specifically to meet your individual needs.

ingrained simply by the repeated use of the wrong clubs.

According to Pat Lange, LPGA Pro and founder of Lange Golf, a custom club manufacturer for women, "The biggest handicap that most women have in this game is the inappropriate equipment they've been forced to play with." And the research shows that it's not long before you learn to live with the mis-fit, although it can be a very unhappy marriage.

Right or wrong you'll adjust

Expert fitter Ross Henry's research has shown that amateur golfers tend to adjust themselves to their ill-fit equipment. "I can give you any club and you'll figure a way to hit it. If you believe the club is right and you're wrong, you'll change your swing. What always happens is that amateurs match themselves to the club they happen to have in their hand. And that's one of the big differences between amateurs and professional golfers. Professionals can take any club a manufacturer gives them and hit it a few times. When they're sure they're making their good, balanced swing, and the ball doesn't go where it's supposed to go, they throw the club away. The amateur does just the opposite. They pick a club and adjust their swing to it and say, 'Well, this club must work; I paid $500 for it.' So the perception with most amateurs is that they are the ones who are wrong, not the equipment."

As teachers we see this all the time in our golf schools. A student has a new set of "off the rack" clubs and is determined to adjust to the clubs even if it ruins their swing in the process. One woman in the school had a brand new set of clubs that were much too stiff and two inches too long for her. When told that she was mis-fit she said that the next time she bought clubs she would be

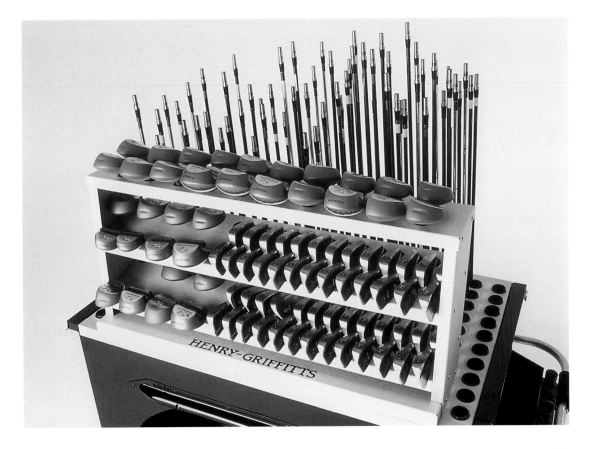

Custom club fitters can adjust each element of the club to suit your swing and body build, so that your equipment enhances your swing. Improperly fit equipment can actually cause swing errors to occur.

Right or wrong you'll adjust *continued*

custom fit. We asked when that would be and she said at least two years down the road. So for the next two years she'll play with clubs that teach her to swing incorrectly and by the time she gets the correct clubs she'll have learned to swing perfectly—perfectly wrong!

Another problem women face, especially the stronger player, is the lack of variety in women's clubs. Although it's changing, manufacturers historically have focused most of their attention on the male side of the market. Recently, as the number of women golfers has increased, variety in women's clubs is starting to arrive.

Sandy Jaskol, promotions manager at Titleist, reports that her company is clarifying the perfor-

mance needs of serious women golfers through club and shaft research projects and test opportunities. Appropriate lofts, lie angles and shaft flex options are being determined through a combination of resources, including input from Titleist and Foot-Joy Worldwide's Women's Advisory Board and Panel Members, which consists of LPGA and PGA Women Golf Professionals nationwide, computerized testing and focus group surveys and studies. Jaskol says, "Research attained from shaft flex performance preferences, in addition to shaft and club color and graphics surveys from serious women golfers, is positively influencing our current direction in customization for women through custom fitting."

Club manufacturers, such as Titleist, are now broadening their research into women's equipment. Here, their Women's Advisory Board, comprised of female golf professionals, discuss the equipment specifications for women.

General guidelines

In this chapter, you'll learn how the individual specifications of a golf club affect your ability to swing and ultimately the quality of your ball flight. There are five important features that affect performance: shaft flex; weight; length; lie angle; and grip size. You'll also learn about components such as club head styles and shaft materials.

Five important club specifications

1 Shaft flex

Incorrect shaft flex is probably the most common characteristic of misfit clubs and the most harmful to your golf swing. The shaft is often referred to as "the engine of the club," but if the shafts in your clubs are wrong for you they're no more useful to you than a car without gasoline. When your shafts are too stiff, you'll struggle to get the club head back to the ball and hang on your back foot to help the ball into the air. When your shafts are too flexible, you'll find it hard to be consistent with your direction as well as the trajectory of your shot.

A properly fit shaft does three things for you:
1 It adds a powerful kick to your shots.
2 It returns your club face square at impact.
3 It allows you to swing in balance.

Pat Lange says that she "found early on that there was not a shaft made for women that seemed to be flexible enough for a certain population of female players," so that was the first product she developed when she began her custom club making business.

Shaft flex is the mysterious element in the fitting process. The popular belief that shaft flex is determined by swing speed, which is largely dependent on physical strength, does not always hold true. Surprisingly, when all elements are

taken into consideration, a tour player may need the same shaft flex as a non-athletic woman who doesn't have much strength. The point is that matching shaft flex to swing speed as the sole fitting parameter is dangerous.

Club head speed While not the only bench mark, club head speed is a good starting point for finding the right shaft for your clubs. It's defined as the speed of the head just a few inches before impact measured in miles per hour. For those who swing the club slowly (under 60 mph), the most flexible shafts should suit you best. These shafts are usually marked with an "F" for flexible. Although it's changing, "F" shafts are also known as "ladies' shafts," so sometimes you'll find an "L" on the shaft instead of an "F." They are not, however, suitable for all women and are appropriate for some men.

For golfers who swing a little faster (60 to 80 mph), the slightly less flexible "A" shaft may work best. It's commonly known as a men's "senior shaft" but here again gender and age are really irrelevant. An "R" or regular shaft is the next step up the scale, and is suggested for those who swing from 81 to 94 mph. These shafts are generally the standard for male amateurs but are commonly used by strong female golfers, especially professionals. An "S" on the shaft stands for stiff, and

In choosing your equipment it's a good idea to follow these general guidelines:
1 Whatever your choice of clubs, consult your golf teacher to make sure that your swing is matched well with the clubs that you're going to buy.
2 Don't buy anything unless you are given the opportunity to "try before you buy."
3 Go to a professional fitter and never accept a static fit. A quality fitting procedure is always dynamic, i.e. you're fit with the club in motion.

Golf clubs have come a long way since their original wooden shafts. Now the material of choice is graphite, and with good reason. Graphite and other light-weight materials, such as titanium, have made it possi-ble for manufacturers to move more weight into the club head for higher, more powerful shots. However, steel shafts still have plenty of appeal: they are much less expensive than graphite, and many better players still prefer them, especially in their irons, because they are more accurate. But if distance is your problem and money isn't, go for the graphite or titanium.

When clubs are too heavy, they commonly cause golfers to make too long a backswing, where the club drops past parallel. Since the club head has traveled a great distance from the ball, returning the club to the ball with power and accuracy is a struggle for most golfers.

General guidelines *continued*

"XS" for extra stiff. These are the least flexible shafts and a high swing speed is required to make them flex and kick into the ball correctly.

It's worth repeating that, while important, swing speed is only one variable in the mix. The only way to get the right fit is to undergo a hands-on fit by an expert who can interpret all the variables.

2 Club weight

One of the most common swing errors among women is the "over- swing," where you lose con-trol of the club allowing the club shaft to drop past the proper parallel position at the top of your swing. A common cause of over-swinging is using clubs that are too heavy.

In the past, swing weight (the relation of the length of the club to the weight in the head measured in ounces/inches) was the key concept with designations like C8, D0 and D4, but now space-age computers show us that the focus should be on the club with a light "dead weight," i.e. the actual weight of the club when measured in ounces.

3 Length

You'll learn in Chapter 2 on set up that good posture and good balance go hand in hand. But if your clubs are not the correct length for you, you'll be forced into an unbalanced position over the ball. Clubs that are too short force an upright plane, one that's too abrupt. Clubs that are too long flatten your swing arc because you must stand too far away from the ball. If you start out of balance at address you'll struggle to regain balance throughout your swing. Since no one likes to fall over, you'll naturally be more concerned with keeping your balance than hitting the ball.

The length of the club also affects the centeredness of contact, so if you want to hit the ball squarely, producing a shot that feels light and effortless, your clubs need to be the proper length. Lange's statistics show that "for every half-inch you hit off-center with an iron you lose approximately five percent in distance, and with woods, it's anywhere from five to seven percent." The point is that you can't just add length to your clubs and expect to get more distance.

If your clubs are too short and you make a good swing, you'll make contact with the ball on the toe. If your clubs are too long, you'll hit in by the heel. Thus you can see the cycle that develops with mis-fit clubs: you make a good swing and hit the ball on the heel. The club head twists open causing a weak shot to the right. You think you've made a bad swing so on the next swing you make some changes—you might strengthen an already correct grip or you take the club more to the inside

Since the tall golfer at the rear is using clubs that are too short, she must bend excessively to the ball. The near golfer is using clubs that are too long, as evidenced by her erect posture.

Face tape can determine the area of the club face that contacts the ball. If your clubs are the right length, it helps you to hit the solid center of the club face each time.

General guidelines *continued*

Your driver is designed to hit the ball longer than any of your other clubs not only because it has the least amount of loft, but also because it has the longest shaft. The trend these days is to make clubs with longer shafts, especially drivers, because the longer the shaft the further your club head travels during your swing and that spells power. Unfortunately, you'll reach a point where the longer the club the more difficult it is to make solid contact—a prerequisite for a powerful shot. The only way to determine how long you can go is to hit clubs of varying lengths and compare them.

Long-shafted drivers help you gain distance only if you can deliver the club face squarely to the ball. If the shaft is too long for you, you'll have trouble making solid contact, in which case your distance can actually decrease.

thereby ruining your take away. By the time you finish, you've gone from a good swing-bad clubs scenario to a bad swing-bad clubs situation.

As we have said, the only way you can be sure that the length of a set of clubs is right for you is to test them dynamically. Either you or your golf professional can apply a special tape to the face of the club, so that when you hit the ball it leaves a mark on the face. After 10 or 15 balls a clear pattern should develop, ideally in the center of the club face.

4 Grips

Getting the correct grip size is important for distance because the right-sized grip facilitates the releasing action of the club so that you generate as much force as possible and still control the club. When your grip is too large, it prevents you from releasing the club on time; on the other hand, play with too small a grip and you'll overuse your hands giving your swing that flippy look.

The size of your grip should be fit to the size of your hand. To be sure you have the right-sized grip make sure that the tip of your left hand ring finger just barely touches the heel pad of your left hand when you're gripping the club properly (see page 23). If there's a large gap, your grips are too big, and if one or more of your fingers is digging into your heel pad, your grips are too small. You'll find ladies', men's and seniors grips but ignore the labels and get what's right for you.

The material in your grips affects the feel, and the texture of grips is a personal preference. Some people like a smooth, leathery feel while others like the more textured feel of a cord grip. A word of caution: if you play golf in hot, humid conditions, a textured grip, such as the cord, is less likely to slip in your hands.

Golf grips are relatively inexpensive but often golfers neglect to replace them once they wear out. Grips age rapidly, not only because of use but also due to deterioration from the extreme heat they suffer in car trunks. And unless you are conscientious about cleaning them on a regular basis,

Worn grips can make you hold your club too tightly, and this tension can actually turn a good swing into a bad one.

sunscreens and lotions build up and make them slick. All these combine to make grips slippery and difficult to control.

One solution is to keep your grips clean by washing them with warm soapy water, then rinsing and drying them. Also avoid storing them in your car where they are exposed to extreme temperatures, and, of course, have them replaced once they're worn.

Note: the markings on the grip are not guides of how you should position your hands. Thus when you take your grip on the club be sure to ignore the markings on the grip.

5 Lie angle

All clubs are built with the toe slightly in the air to account for the in-swing bending of the shaft toward the ground. The angle at which the shaft is drilled into the neck of the club depends on the individual fit. If your swing is sound but you're still troubled by off-line shots you should have your lies checked.

When your club sits properly on the ground the sole is flush, the face aims straight ahead, and the loft is correct. For this to happen, your clubs must have the correct lie angle—a specification that varies depending on the individual.

You can use a piece of sole tape to check the lie angle of your club (see page 18 for some expect advice on how to do this).

Flat and upright When you set up to the ball with good posture and the toe of your club is too much off the ground your club face actually aims to the left of the target, so you'll need to have your clubs "flatted" by lowering the toe. And if the heel is up in the air when you're in a good

Your divots
tell tales

Even if you don't have a lie board you'll know your lie angle is off from your divots. If your divots are consistently "toe deep," meaning they're deeper where the toe passed through the ground, your lie is too flat. If they're heel deep, your clubs are too upright. Instead of changing your golf swing, have your clubs adjusted to the proper lie angle so that your good swings are rewarded with good shots.

General guidelines *continued*

address position, your club face aims to the right. Your clubs should be more upright, i.e. the toe should be raised more off the ground.

Most golf professionals have access to a machine that adjusts clubs to the proper lie angle by bending the shaft near the neck of your club. To test the lie, your golf professional or club fitter tapes the sole of your club and you hit balls from what is known as a lie board. If the lie angle is correct, the tape will be marked in the center of the sole from its contact with the board, and if the lie is incorrect the evidence will be on the tape.

In addition to getting these elements of your clubs properly matched to meet your needs, you'll have other choices to make regarding the design of your club heads. These "game improvement" options can help you add distance and accuracy to your golf game.

Club head design

While there are other combinations, most simply iron club heads come in two basic styles: forged or cast. Their names refer to the process used to manufacture them; whereas the forged club head is pounded into shape, the cast is made from a mold. Forged irons are also known as "muscle backs" because their weight is focused in the center of the club face—known as the sweet spot. Cast heads are known as "perimeter weighted" because their weight is evenly distributed from the heel to the toe of the club.

Forged versus cast

The problem with forged clubs is that contact on the toe or heel doesn't have a lot of weight behind it so the ball doesn't go as far as a centered hit. These off-center hits also cause the face to twist and your shots to go off line. Perimeter-weighted clubs are far more forgiving of mis-hits because the sweet spot is actually bigger since the weight distribution allows much less twisting for off-center hits.

If you're confident that you can hit the sweet spot the majority of the time you'll enjoy the soft feel of forged heads and the ease with which you can draw and fade the ball. If, like most golfers, you tend to hit the ball inconsistently you'll benefit from the greater margin of error cast heads allow.

Over-sized heads

Nowadays new, light-weight materials allow irons and woods to be made with over-sized heads. Like an over-sized tennis racket, you've got a larger area to contact and the lighter material allows greater distribution of weight for an even larger sweet spot.

Despite their generic name, today most woods are made of metal or light-weight materials, such as graphite and titanium. Again, these newer materials allow greater weight distribution for larger sweet spots. The trend with woods is bigger heads with game improvement features. Our experience of watching thousands of students with these over-sized heads is that they really do help them play better golf and are therefore a worthwhile investment.

Offset heads

Irons and, more recently, woods are offered in an "offset" style where the leading edge of the club is behind or "offset" from the hosel. This feature helps to get the ball in the air more easily. If you're a low ball hitter, test out the offset feature. If you already hit the ball high enough, stay with the standard design.

The driver on the left features an oversized head, whereas the driver on the right has a jumbo head. Like oversized and jumbo tennis rackets, these drivers provide you with a larger hitting area and an expanded sweet spot, thereby providing more solid contact to off-center hits.

Putting it all together

Once you have the right club specifications for your long game you're ready to choose the individual clubs that will make up your set. According to The Rules of Golf you can have up to 14 clubs in your bag. Making smart choices here can take strokes off your handicap.

Putters

Putters are made in three basic styles: the box, the blade and the mallet. The box putter features perimeter weighting, like cast irons, which give you a bigger sweet spot and, therefore, more margin for error if you hit slightly off center. Blade putters, preferred by golfers with very consistent putting strokes, have the majority of weight in the center of the club face. Mis-hits are more likely to roll off line but centered hits roll straight and true. The mallet putter often features a heavy head. Golfers who struggle with excess hand motion and have short, abrupt putting strokes find that the weight of the mallet keeps the club head swinging and helps them make more of a "stroking" motion. Mallets are also helpful on slow greens because the weight of the head tends to roll the ball firmly without excess motion.

The long putter

Pendulum putters, featuring a shaft that extends about chest high, can be found with every variety of club head. Since you can anchor the top of the long shaft against your chest with your left hand and move it with your right hand, the golfer who struggles with excessive wrist action can find relief with this style of putter. These putters tend to be especially good on short putts, because the stroke is very stable, but on long putts you may have difficulty with distance control. The key to the long putter is patience because it takes about two weeks of practice to get used to it, but once you're over the breaking-in hurdle, it can be very effective.

Note: if you play a course with severely undulating greens, stay away from the long putter—it's too hard to handle on big slopes.

You should choose a putter head that complements your putting ability and the type of greens you play most often.

Long irons versus utility woods

Old habits die hard and it's tough to imagine not carrying a three, four and five iron but the trend is definitely toward utility woods, and not just among amateurs. Liselotte Neumann, winner of the 1988 US Open, carries a variety of woods, including a nine wood, and no irons longer than a six iron. Annika Sorenstam, 1995 and 1996 US Open Champion, also uses a nine wood.

Pat Lange says, "I think a seven wood should be in most women's golf bags. We've renamed our seven wood '911' because, in any emergency, this club comes to your rescue. We make our seven wood with a four or five wood length, but the loft gives confidence to anyone who has qualms about getting the ball airborne. Most women generally don't like hitting long irons, so the three and four irons are not even considered for most women's sets."

We predict that the day isn't far off where a nine, ten and even an eleven wood will be standard in a set of clubs. They are easier to hit, and out of the rough these woods perform much better than their iron counterparts.

Wedges

In Chapter 8 on bunker play you'll learn how a club with special features (the sand wedge) is your best choice in a green side bunker, but a sand wedge can be a stroke saver in various green side situations other than sand. Since it's the heaviest club in your bag, it cuts through thick rough much easier than your other clubs. Your sand wedge also has the most loft, so your shots fly high and land softly, a necessity in those situations when you don't have much putting surface to hit to. The lob wedge, which is even more lofted than your sand wedge, should be in every golfer's bag. Once you get comfortable with it even those treacherous green side shots over bunkers can be executed with ease.

Three wedges can add some variety to the trajectory of your pitch shots without having to modify your swing.

21

Chapter two

Your set up

How you hold your golf club and aim it, and how you position your body in relation to your target and the golf ball are known as your set up. When you set up to the ball correctly, your odds of making a good swing dramatically increase. For every set up error you commit, you'll have to make a compensating move during your golf swing. The good news is that to make a good set up you don't need any special athletic talents, or any

When you set up to the ball correctly, as shown here, you are well on your way toward making a good golf swing.

previous golf experience. Once you know the details of a correct set up, you can put yourself in a position that gives you the best chance to make a good swing every time you address a ball. If you use the guidelines that follow, each swing you make will be set up for success.

Your grip

The importance of taking your grip correctly is foremost in your set up since your hands control the club face. As the world's best players have demonstrated, there are many variations of a golf grip, but there are some mistakes that can be made when gripping a golf club that don't qualify as variations as explained below.

These mistakes occur when a beginner places her hands on the club in a manner that feels most comfortable at address, usually high into the palms of each hand. Although this grip feels powerful, it provides almost no support for the club during the golf swing and restricts the wrists to the point where they are unable to contribute the power they provide in a good swing. If you learn to play golf with this grip, you will develop a swing that has an up-and-down look, because your faulty grip forced you to lift the golf club up without coiling. When your grip is correct, it helps you swing the club and elevate it with the turn of your body and the hinging of your wrists.

Don't confuse comfort and correct

The first hurdle in learning a correct golf grip is not to mistake what is comfortable with what is actually correct. A golf grip may not feel comfortable at first but because it supports your club throughout your swing, coupled with the powerful action it allows in your wrists, you'll get accustomed to your new grip quite quickly.

Although it might feel comfortable at address, this grip causes irreparable swing errors and powerless golf shots.

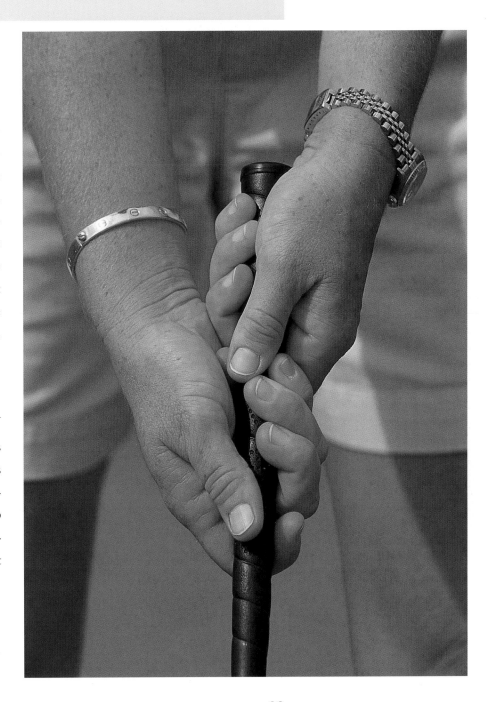

Your grip *continued*

Taking your grip

Placement of the left hand

Rather than placing your hands on the club with the club head resting on the ground, we recommend that you hold the club up in front of you to take your grip as a safeguard against some common grip errors.

1   Start with your right arm fully extended in front of you, holding the club in your right hand with the shaft at a 45-degree angle to your body.

2   Now extend your left arm out to meet the club, making sure that your left arm is above rather than beside your chest.

3   Without changing the angle of the club, place the side of the grip (rather than the under belly of the grip) across the base of the palm of your left hand. Set at the proper angle: the grip runs at a slight diagonal, from the top of your left index finger across the base of your palm.

4   Then simply close your left hand around the club. Your left thumb should end up slightly to the right of the center of the grip

Placement of the right hand

1   While holding your club in your left hand, with your left arm extended in front of you, extend your right pinkie (little) finger outward, and place the middle segments of your two middle fingers on the underside of the grip.

2   Slide these fingers up the shaft until they lightly contact your left hand.

3   Now close your right palm over your left thumb. Your right index finger also closes around the club, very close to your middle finger.

4   Lastly, let your pinkie finger fall into place approximately over the ridge between your left index and middle fingers.

1   Place the side of the grip against the base of the fingers of your left hand.

2   Place your left thumb between the pocket formed by your right thumb and heel pad.

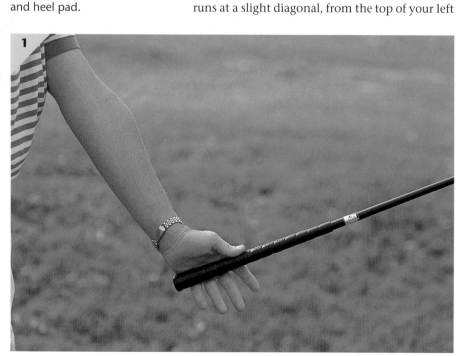

You will find this method helpful for the following reasons:

■ Presetting your left arm on top of your chest insures that you can swing your arm across your chest to start your swing without any restrictions. This allows for maximum club head arc without losing the important connection of your left arm and chest. If you place your left hand on the grip with the club head on the ground your left arm gets stuck beside your chest. You may see thin-chested male players with their left arm to the side of the chest at address, but men are built differently from women, and for a woman this position either causes a very restricted, powerless swing or, more often, a lift of the left arm off the chest to gain freedom of movement, which robs you of both power and accuracy.

■ When you hold the club up in front of you to take your grip, the club head is at eye level. From this position, it is easy to see if you are gripping the club with the club face square. Your check point is that the leading edge of the club (the bottom edge of the club face) is in line with the center line of your body.

■ If the leading edge forms a line that starts more toward your right shoulder and ends by your left hip, your club face will point to the right when you address the ball.

■ If the line of the leading edge goes in the opposite direction, your club face will aim left at address.

■ The 45-degree angle is the correct angle at which the club needs to be placed into your left hand. Many golfers incorrectly grip the club too

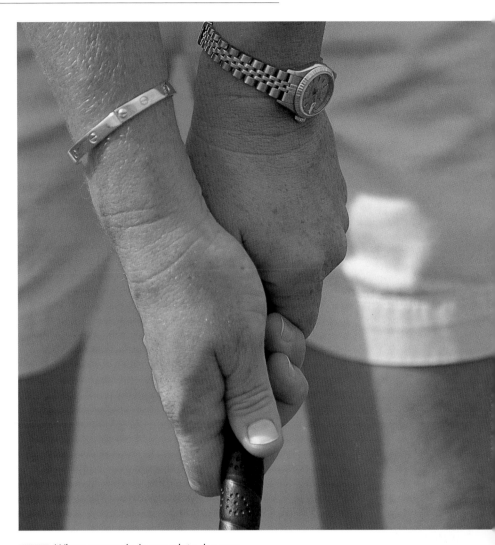

When your grip is complete, be sure that the "V's" formed by your thumbs and forefinger point just inside your right shoulder, never at your left.

high into the palm of the left hand so that the club shaft forms a straight line with the left arm. When the club head is resting on the ground in front of you, it should form a 45-degree angle with your left arm—the same angle you created as the first step of your grip assembly.

Grip
variations

There are three grip variations determined by how you place the smallest finger (your pinkie) of your right hand on the club.

1 The grip described on page 24 is known as the overlap, since the pinkie overlaps your left index finger, hooking around the joint located just below your index knuckle that bends the finger.

2 The interlock weaves the right pinkie and the left index as they wrap around one another. The interlocked fingers should meet at about your knuckles to maintain the club more in the fingers of each hand. If you choose the interlock grip be careful not to weave these fingers so that the base of your palms touch each other. One of the dangers of this grip is the tendency to force the club too high into the palms, thereby preventing the correct hinging of the wrists.

3 The ten-finger, or baseball, grip can be effective if you have limited strength and/or trouble cocking your wrists. Use the method described for the overlap grip except don't overlap with your pinkie. Instead, allow all of your fingers to rest on the club.

Your grip *continued*

Check points for a good grip

1 Locate the two tendons of your left thumb by moving your thumb toward your body. The area where they disappear into your wrist forms a depression we call the "snuff box" and it is your guide to a perfect grip.

2 To be sure that your left wrist joint is directly on top of the club rather than to one side, simply place your snuff box directly over the center of the handle of your club.

3 Check to make sure that the heel pad of your left hand (not the thumb pad) rests on top of the grip. You should feel that the club is held in the fingers of your right hand and that your left thumb fits in the pocket formed by your right thumb pad and heel pad. If you've done this, the palm of your right hand aims in the same direction as your club face, at the target.

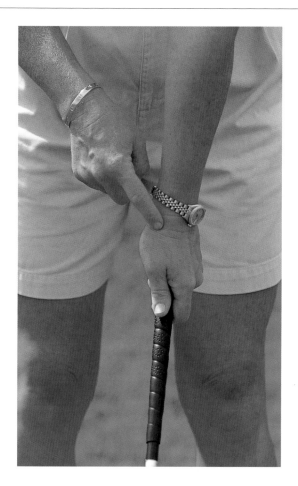

Posture

To establish good posture, take your grip as described above. Stand erect, with your left arm on top of, rather than beside, your chest. With your arms hanging comfortably from your shoulders and the club shaft held horizontal to the ground, simply let the club head drop to the ground as you bend forward from your hip sockets. Now flex your knees slightly for comfort and balance.

Be careful not to push your knees out toward the ball. From here, assuming the correct posture is a two step process:

■ Firstly, let your hips bend your upper body forward, pushing your weight toward your toes.

■ Secondly, let your knees bend your body backward until your weight settles across the arches of your feet.

When you've done this correctly, your rear end sticks out behind you, and your knees,

Even though good golf requires that you bend from the hips, which results in a protruding tail end, many women are reluctant to do so for reasons of comportment. Rest assured that on the golf course, this posture is accepted as the norm. Remember that you have to bend to the ball because it's on the ground. If you only bend from your waist, your weight falls to your toes and you'll lose your balance as you swing. Bending from the hips creates a counter balance: the weight of your upper body bent forward is balanced by the weight of your lower body behind rather than under you. The larger your upper body, the more you'll have to create a counter balance with your lower body.

although they are flexed, are over your shoelaces, not over your toes.

Posture check

You can check this out in a mirror. If your posture is correct you'll see that an imaginary line connects the top of your spine, the tips of your elbows, tips of your knees and the balls of your feet. Your weight should be balanced from in the middle of your feet—never out on your toes or completely back on your heels.

1 With your left arm hanging atop your chest, hold the club shaft parallel to the ground. Bend forward from your hips, not your waist, and let the club head drop toward the ground. Then flex your knees for comfort.

2 Though it varies somewhat for different individual body types, correct posture creates a vertical line connecting the top of your spine, tips of your elbows, tips of your knees and balls of your feet.

Stance width

If your posture is good, with your weight balanced across the middle of your feet, you should wind up at a proper distance from the ball as a result. Once you've addressed the ball you can check it by taking your right hand off the club and spreading your fingers. You should be able to pass your right hand between your left hand and your body. If there is room for more than one hand, your weight is probably out on your toes because you've bent over too much from your hips. If your hand cannot pass through this gap, then your weight is probably on your heels because you've flexed your knees excessively and neglected to bend from your hips.

Your stance width will vary according to the length of the club that you are using.

■ For your medium to short irons (5-PW), your feet should be no further than hip distance apart. But be careful: the width of your feet should be measured from your heels rather than your toes. If you flare your feet outward and use your toes as a guide you may miss the fact that your heels are only a few inches apart—too narrow a platform to support the movement of your body throughout your golf swing.

■ For your longer irons, fairway woods and driver, your stance should be shoulder width to accommodate the wider swing arc that the shaft length of these clubs demands.

Stance width test

To be sure your stance width is correct, use the following test. Take what you think is the appropriate stance and make a golf swing.

■ When you finish your swing, if your knees end up even with each other, then you know that your stance width is correct.

■ If there is a large gap between your knees then your stance is too wide.

■ If your right knee passes your left, you will know that your stance is too narrow.

1 With an iron, your stance should be about hip width apart, as measured from the insides of your feet.

2 With a driver, your stance should be about shoulder width, as measured from the insides of your feet.

Ball position

As with the width of your stance, where you position the ball between your feet varies depending on the club you use.

■ With your medium to short irons (6 through PW), position the ball slightly forward of the center of your stance. Since ball position can be distorted by the flare of your feet, it's good to have an upper body reference to make sure you've got the position correct. The corresponding position in reference to your upper body is that the ball is off your left cheek.

■ For your long irons and fairway woods, you should move the ball one ball width forward or off the left side of your chest, where a logo on your shirt usually appears.

■ For your driver and all teed woods, move the ball one more ball width forward, opposite your left heel and your left underarm.

Foot flare

How much you flare your feet at address depends on your ability to turn back and through the ball. To establish a starting point, take a few normal strides and then notice the position of your feet when you stop walking. Use this as your starting point when taking your stance. The average flare is about one-quarter of a turn from perpendicular, so step in with your feet pointing directly at the target line, then turn them out to a 25-degree angle.

If you have difficulty turning behind the ball, due to limited flexibility or a large upper body, flare your right foot out to increase your freedom of movement.

If you're an experienced player and you hit a lot of shots weak to the right, reduce the flare of your left foot. If you hit a lot of shots low and to the left, increase the flare of your right foot.

Your upper body can provide an additional check point for correct ball position. For example, medium to short irons are played slightly forward of the center of your stance or just off your left cheek.

Aim and alignment

Note: in the jargon of instruction, it is possible to have your shoulders open, your hips closed and your feet square, so when you check your body lines check them all. Golfers often make the mistake of aiming their body lines at the target instead of parallel left of it. In this case, the club face usually aims right of the target and the body is in a closed position. Only a well-manipulated swing can direct this shot to the target, but to do so consistently will be all but impossible. Remember: in golf you aim your club face and align your body.

1 Place the leading edge of your club perpendicular to your target line to aim your club face correctly.

2 Align your body parallel left of your target.

In golf, aim and alignment are two words that are often confused. When this happens, you'll have difficulty not only with your direction but also your golf swing. When you aim your club face incorrectly, and position your body in poor alignment, you'll be left with no other choice but to over-manipulate your swing to get the ball to your target. With good aim and alignment, your direction is established before you swing and your swing is dedicated to producing the proper distance.

■ Remember that only the club face aims at the target, and your body aligns square to your target line. To aim your club face correctly, place the leading edge of the club perpendicular to your target line, an imaginary line extending from your ball to your target. If your club face points to the right of your target, your club face is open; if it points to the left, it's closed.

■ Next, align your body square to your target line. This means that imaginary lines connecting your feet, hips and shoulders are parallel left of your target line. The often used comparison to a rail road track is a good one: your club face is on the outer track and the lines of your body run down the inner track. When your body lines point at the target, your body is in what is known as a closed position, and if your body points at an angle left of your target, you are in an open position.

30

Pre-shot routine

The process you go through before every shot brings together all the aspects of your set up, especially aim and alignment. If you are diligent about building a good set up, you will also develop a strong pre-shot routine. The elements of your set up become so routine that there is no chance of forgetting something because they have become ingrained and thus a habit. Your pre-shot routine can be your best friend because when the pressure is on and your mind is racing, you can make the correct plan and build a good set up automatically.

To make it a habit, go through the process of building your set up exactly the same way for each shot you hit in your practice. Before you know it, you won't even think about taking your grip, your stance, posture or ball position, and this frees you to focus on your target.

The routine itself

1   Always approach each ball from behind, looking down your intended target line. From this position you'll have the best look at your target. Once you've gotten a good image of the direction you want your ball to travel, pick a specific target where you want it to land.

2   Then pick a distinct marker in the distance—a tree, fence post, bunker or rooftop, on an extension past your target. If you just pick a spot of grass on the fairway, you run the risk of losing it when you look away to address your ball.

3   Draw an imaginary line back from your distant target, over your landing area, and back to the front of the tee box. Now, pick out a close-up target on your line: a divot, an old tee or some other mark. Tee your ball so that it is in line with this close-up target.

4   When you walk into your ball, set your club face square to your close-up target and then set your body square to your club face. When you look back from your set up position to

confirm your target in the fairway, you'll recognize it immediately with the help of your more obvious distant target.

A good routine *speeds up play*

As you can see, a good pre-shot routine is an important element in playing better golf. But sometimes, in an effort not to be accused of slow play, golfers rush their shots. Women are particularly susceptible to this because the men in this male-dominated sport have a habit of erroneously labeling women as slow players despite the fact that studies show that women are no more guilty of slow play than men.

Still, the intimidation factor is there when a group of men playing behind you posture themselves with their hands on their hips. Our advice is to ignore them and go through your normal routine. If you hurry and break your pre-shot pattern, you'll probably hit a bad shot and then you will play slowly because you'll take more swings. A good routine, from the time you tee the ball until the time you hit the ball, should take you no more than 30 to 45 seconds. If you take longer than that, you are slow and you should reduce the time of your routine.

31

Chapter three

Your golf swing

According to the USGA the average woman golfer hits her tee shot about 130 yards so that even on courses with shorter forward tees, this average woman is still at a disadvantage distance-wise. Therefore this chapter on swing mechanics not only gives you the tools for a sound golf swing but it focuses on the keys to gaining distance.

Special attention is also given to the differences between a woman's swing and a man's swing. However, please remember that these differences are not a negative factor. Indeed, since so many instructional materials focus on men's swings, the differences in a woman's shape

LPGA Hall of Fame member Patty Sheehan has one of golf's finest swings.

and strength level need to be specifically addressed to play better golf.

Body shape and swing

In the past, women's breasts were thought to be a detriment to their golf swing because, to maintain connection of the left arm to the body, your left arm must slide uninterrupted across the top of your chest. However, a woman's physique is not the problem; the real problem is that women are often taught the wrong set up position.

In the past, both men and women were instructed to let their arms hang down naturally at address, a position that puts your arms at the sides of your chest—exactly wrong for women (and for big-chested men). Most men can swing their left arm across their chest with no interruption. But for a woman, letting her arms hang at her sides places her left arm beside her breast, leaving her two options: restrict her arm swing, thereby limiting her swing arc and power, or lift her arms above her chest, thereby losing the power of connection. Neither option is good.

As a woman you need to set your left arm on top of your chest at address so that your arm can swing freely across your chest. This way, regardless of the size of your breasts, you can stay connected to your body with a wide swing arc.

Upper body strength

Although there are exceptions, generally women have less upper body strength than men. However, this does not preclude you from having a powerful golf swing, if you make maximum use of the mechanics in your golf swing that produce distance with good direction: coil, leverage, and an on-plane swing.

Coil

Coil is the amount your shoulders turn in relationship to your legs and hips. If you have had any instruction at all you've probably been taught to turn your body behind the ball, but you may not have been taught to coil. There is a difference.

Powerful coil in your backswing is built as your left arm swings across your chest, your shoulders turn against your hips and your hips turn against your firmly-planted lower body. At the top of your backswing, your hips should be turned about twice as much as your lower legs, and your shoulders twice as much as your hips. The exact percentage (e.g. 45 degrees of hip turn and 90 degrees of shoulder turn) does not matter nearly as much as the ratio (in our example, 2:1).

The main ingredient in creating distance is a powerful coil. Coil is produced when your shoulders turn about twice the distance your hips do in your backswing.

Upper body strength *continued*

When you create your maximum ratio, you will feel the muscles of your legs and back wound up and ready to explode into the ball, like a sling shot that has been stretched back and is ready to fire.

Problems occur when the hips and shoulders turn back an equal amount with no differential, usually aggravated by the left foot lifting off the ground. In this case, there's plenty of turn but no coil, and you can't hit the ball very far without coil. A big turn with no coil has a loose feeling, as though not much is happening, and it isn't. The sling shot is available but since it hasn't been stretched, no power is generated.

Leverage

Another element of power is leverage: the angles you create between your body and your golf club.

Levers are multipliers of power and the human body is equipped with powerful levers that can be an integral part of your golf swing if you use them correctly. Leverage in golf is produced by the cocking and uncocking of your wrists and the bending of your right elbow, creating a 90-degree angle between your left arm and the club shaft. By cocking your wrists, you elevate the club to the top of your backswing with minimal exertion as you maintain the powerful connection of your arms to your body.

Unfortunately, your club can also be elevated incorrectly by lifting your arms off your chest, your left foot off the ground, and straightening your spine. In this scenario, little coil is produced and the benefits of leverage are minimized. To make use of the power of leverage, you'll hinge your wrists and bend your right elbow while

1 If your wrists remain un-hinged at this point in your backswing, the club is in a very heavy position.

2 By hinging your wrists you employ the power of leverage, put the club in a light position, and multiply your potential for power.

Three elements of ball control

As we have seen, coil produces the power, leverage multiplies it and saves it for impact, and the correct swing plane insures that the power is expended in the direction of the target. On the following pages are the actual mechanics that are conducive to producing these three vital elements and impart the correct distance and direction to your golf shots.

you maintain your golf posture and build coil with the big muscles of your legs and back.

Plane

The plane of your swing is established by the angle your club shaft creates with the ground at address. You'll want your club to return to impact at the same angle you established at address so your club face aims at the target. When your club shaft matches the angle established at address throughout your backswing and downswing, it's called an on-plane swing. This is a very accurate way to make a golf swing as you'll see in the Star Swings section (see page 50).

1 When your club is properly soled at address, the angle of the shaft establishes the plane of your golf swing.

2 Though the club shaft is inverted, a proper backswing places the shaft at the same angle it established at address, as indicated by the white pole.

3 Through the swing the club shaft once again matches the plane established at address.

Your golf swing in detail

In order to describe the details of your golf swing it is necessary to break them down into individual pieces. Please remember, however, that your golf swing is a blending of these motions and cannot actually be executed piece by piece when you are on the golf course. They can be learned one piece at a time on the driving range but, when you play, you'll need to stop thinking in pieces and let your motion be one of a well-coordinated swing.

The takeaway

From a proper set up position, you are ready to start your takeaway—the movement of the club away from the ball.

1   To do so, let your left arm swing across your chest until it begins to pull your left shoulder behind the ball. As your left arm swings, your right arm moves away from your right side and your right elbow begins to fold.

2   Just before your hands reach hip level, you'll begin to cock your wrists. When you do, your hands remain low as your club head gets high and slightly behind your toe line.

Caution: a common error during the takeaway is to roll your hands and forearms, causing your club

face to open (point to the sky at hip height) and the club head to get deep behind you. From this position, your only option is to lift the club to the top, thereby destroying your coil and the path of your swing.

Check your takeaway

To be sure you've made it through your takeaway correctly, check the following points.

1 Lay a club shaft on an extension of the line of your toes away from the target. From the time you start your takeaway your hands should stay on your toe line, neither moving inside or outside the line.

2 When your left arm reaches a position where it is parallel to the ground, check that your hands are still on your toe line.

3 At this point your right elbow is bent, creating a right angle between your forearm and your upper arm, with your wrists cocked so your club head is high but your hands are low. The club should now be in a very light position supported by the pedestal of your hands. The leverage of your golf swing is now set.

Check your swing plane

From a well-executed takeaway position you will start to feel coil building in the muscles of your left side, especially the back of your left forearm. As the motion of your left arm across your chest drags your left shoulder away from its address position, you'll also feel coil as your feet remain planted. At this point, you can check the plane of your swing.

The shaft of your club should form the

When your left arm swings to a position parallel to the ground, check that your hands are still over your toe line and the butt end of your club points at an extension of your target line.

same angle with the ground that it did at address, i.e. the butt end of your club points at an extension of your target line back from the ball, with your hands on your toe line. You are now ready to elevate the club to the top of your swing.

As you can see, your backswing is controlled by a combination of arm swing and shoulder turn, but there are several other important elements. Your hips play a significant role in the backswing, moving in response to the motion of your upper body. Your hips turn until your right hip is over your right heel, and no further, making their journey a short one. At the top of your swing you should feel about 80 to 90 percent of your weight in your right hip, knee, and foot, with the weight balanced from the ball of your right foot to your heel. To avoid a hip sway, keep the weight more toward the inside, rather than the outside, of your right foot.

Your golf swing in detail *continued*

Over the *top*

A move that gets many golfers in trouble is known as coming over the top, when your shoulders start the downswing by turning level to the ground, usually because of an impulse to throw your club head directly at the ball from the top of your swing. This may be the fastest route for your club head to get back to the ball but it is the least effective way to propel your ball to the target.

During the backswing, your club head transcribed a path gradually inward and outward. To reach the target, you must revisit this path on the way down. Throwing your hands at the ball opens your shoulders too early and pushes the club head well outside the path you established on your backswing.

To the top

From your completed takeaway position you can elevate the club to the top of your swing in one of two ways: lift your arms or continue your shoulder turn.

■   If you lift your arms, you'll destroy your coil and posture, an error that results in a loss of distance and accuracy.

■   The correct choice is to continue your shoulder turn until your left shoulder moves behind the ball. In doing so, you will build maximum coil, maintain your posture and keep your golf swing on plane.

Understanding your shoulder turn

To be sure that your shoulders turn properly, you will need to keep them moving at a 90-degree angle to your spine. When you do this, your left shoulder appears to move down while your right shoulder moves up. Actually your shoulders are making a level turn but because your spine is inclined toward the ball, they appear to tilt.

To understand how your shoulders work, stand in front of a mirror and you'll notice your shoulders form a perpendicular T-line with your spine, level to the ground. Turn your chest to the right and then back to the left so your shoulders remain

perpendicular to your spine and level to the ground. If you bend from the waist into your golf posture and turn your shoulders in the same way, you'll have duplicated the motion required for your golf swing. It is important when you swing to keep your shoulders perpendicular to your spine as they turn both back and through the ball.

The key is not to make any effort to move your left shoulder down to the ball, a swing error known as a shoulder tilt. When you tilt your left shoulder down, your weight stays on your left leg and never gets behind the ball. Another

temptation is to level your shoulders to the ground as you turn in your backswing. This straightens your spine and destroys your posture and relationship to the ball.

Your downswing—it starts with a surrender

The start of your downswing requires two moves performed simultaneously: your left arm swings back down your chest as your weight shifts from your right leg to your left.

Your golf swing in detail *continued*

Just as your left arm swung across and up your chest to begin your backswing, it reverses its path to start your downswing. Since your shoulders elevated your arms in your backswing, your left arm has a descending motion as it moves across your chest—you don't make your left arm come down; you let it come down by surrendering to the pull of gravity. Keep in mind, however, that your shoulders stay in place until your arms drag them around: the sequence starts with the arm drop/weight transfer followed by the hip turn, and lastly the shoulder turn.

The pressure shift from your right to your left is extremely subtle, but after it has been accomplished your hips take over your swing and begin a powerful rotation, with your left hip serving as the axis for the rotation. In order to achieve this, you'll need to have the pressure of your weight on your left hip. Again, this transfer of pressure is a subtle movement which is similar to shifting your weight when dancing.

Impact

When your downswing unfolds as it should, your club head is literally on a collision course with the ball. Once your arms have moved back in front of your chest, your shoulders key your swing motion as they did in your backswing. Now your left shoulder moves forward and upward away from the ground and your right shoulder moves toward the

place your left shoulder occupied under your chin at the completion of your backswing. The rotation of your left hip moving behind you causes your left leg to straighten, providing a firm wall to hit against. At impact, your club face mimics its position at address.

Follow through

Although the follow through happens after the ball has gone, it is still an integral part of your golf swing. A well-executed swing is completed with the head, chest and hips facing the target and all of your weight on your left foot. Your right foot is almost completely off the ground, with the toe of your right shoe serving as a balance point on the ground. Even if the ball doesn't go where you

want it to, you should practice finishing each swing in this full and balanced position.

A good follow through is a result, but if you train yourself to go to that position after each swing, you will help improve the earlier parts of your swing. When you know where you're going, you'll use the proper muscles and motions to get you there. So if you finish incorrectly, take a moment to stand in the correct follow through position and concentrate on getting to this position on your next swing.

Blending

As you can imagine, while you are actually swinging, it would be impossible to think about even a

Sometimes, in an effort to transfer weight to their right side golfers sway rather than turn their hips. When the hips sway, they move laterally, to such an extent that the right hip slides outside the right leg. On the down-swing, the left hip slides too much toward the target so that it is outside the left leg through the hitting zone. The problem is that while all this sliding is going on, coiling and the correct swing path take a back seat, so when you sway your hips, you'll hit a variety of fat and thin shots.

To be sure that your hips are working correctly, plant a shaft or an umbrella next to the outside of your right heel and cross your arms across your chest. Make your back-swing motion. If you sway on your backswing, your hips bump into the shaft.

A common error, especially among beginners, is an effort to lift the ball off the ground and into the air. To do so, they hang on their right side during the down-swing and flip their wrists to try to get under the ball. What's worse is that their effort produces exactly the opposite of their objective: at best, a very low shot due to contact with the middle of the ball or, one of the worst shots in golf, the fat shot. The good news is you don't have to do anything in your golf swing to help the ball into the air. The loft of the club is designed to do that for you. Your objective is to drive the ball forward to the target letting the loft of the club provide the trajectory.

Your golf swing in detail *continued*

few of the many instructions you've learned about the golf swing. What you need to do is to evaluate the area of your swing that is most in need of improvement and then work on that one piece until it becomes a habit. Be sure to eliminate errors in your swing in the order in which they occur. For example, fix a takeaway error before you work on your downswing. Golf swings are an excellent example of cause and effect, so often you'll find that an error late in your swing disappears once you perfect an earlier part of the swing. And this follows through to your set up: most errors are eliminated once you set yourself properly to the ball.

Summary

As you have probably noticed, your downswing is a reverse of your backswing motion.

1   Your left arm swings across your chest and your wrists set the club head up and slightly behind you.

2   When your arm can swing no further, your shoulders begin their rotation around your spine and, finally, your right hip turns over your right heel.

3   To start the downswing, the motion reverses itself. Your left arm moves back down your chest as your weight shifts to your left hip.

4   Once your arms drop, your shoulders will continue the motion through the ball as your left hip moves behind you.

5   To finish your swing, your left elbow begins to bend as your right arm moves past impact across your chest.

6   Your club head releases through the ball and your wrists re-hinge; this is a mirror image of your completed takeaway position.

Drills

Throughout this chapter you will find a progression of drills, starting with the most basic eye-hand co-ordination, and building to more golf-specific drills. If you have never played a sport before, start at the beginning. For those who have higher levels of skill, find out where you fit in the progression and begin from that point.

Hand-eye coordination drills

The bucket drill

A simple drill to enhance your hand-eye coordination is to toss balls into a bucket. To do this you should stand six feet away from a wash bucket and toss balls into the bucket. When you can make eight out of ten, take two steps backward and repeat until you are 20 feet away.

The clap drill

Choose a partner and face each other in your golf posture—be careful not to bang heads. Each person extends their right hand so their palms are facing one another. From this position, take turns gently swinging your right arm back and through as it would in your real golf swing so that your palm meets your partner's palm at impact.
Note: once you have mastered hand-eye co-ordination move on to weight transfer drills.

Weight transfer drills

The "X" drill

■ To learn the proper weight transfer in your golf swing, set up with your feet about hip width apart and lay a club from your right heel to your left toe and a second club from your right toe to your left heel. The two clubs form an "X" with each at a 45-degree angle to the target line.

■ Hold a third club across the top of your thighs and turn your right hip over your right heel so that 80 percent of your weight is supported by your right leg. When the shaft across your thighs

You can also use the "X" drill to check the path of your takeaway and follow through by matching the shaft in your hands to the shafts on the ground.

Drills *continued*

matches the one on the ground your lower body backswing transfer is complete.

■ For your downswing transfer, reverse the process and turn your left hip over your left heel until the shaft on your thighs matches the one on the ground.

Balls in pocket drill

■ Place a golf ball in the front pockets of your pants with the grip end of a club against your belly button.

■ Grip down on the shaft until both your arms are fully extended.

■ Now turn your body while shifting your weight to your right side (as in the "X" drill) until the ball in your right pocket is over your right heel.

■ Turn through the ball so your stomach and

club move as a unit, until the ball in your left pocket is over your left heel.

Note: once you have mastered these drills you are ready to learn the body sequence drills.

Body sequence drills

Path drill

■ Place a tee in the hole at the top of your club's grip and another in the ground where the ball would be. Put two more tees two feet behind and in front of the tee on the ground along the target line.

■ Take your grip and golf posture and set up to the center tee.

■ Extend your right index finger down the shaft and swing the club with your arms only so your club head passes over the rear tee, back over the

1 Use the path drill to learn the rudimentary part of your golf swing.

2 Once you have mastered the path drill, move on to the plane drill.

middle tee and through to the front tee. Throughout this motion, your index finger points at the line formed by the tees.

■ Once you can do this, put a ball on the tee and just let the ball get in the way. Don't try to add any force to hit the ball or you will find you change your path.

Plane drill

■ Using the same set up as in the path drill (opposite), use two clubs to mark the extension of the line of your toes—one out from your left foot toward the target and the other out from your right foot away from the target. Be sure that these shafts form a straight line and are parallel to your target line (the line of the tees).

■ From your address position, swing the club back until your right arm folds and your left arm is parallel to the ground. Your left arm and your hands should be over the shaft extending from your right foot, and the tee in the grip end of your club should point at the target line, specifically the back tee.

■ When you swing your club through, your right arm and your hands should be over the shaft extending from your left foot, and the tee in your club should point at the target line.

1 The plane drill also teaches you how to set the leverage for your golf swing.

2 When done correctly, you'll also learn how to release the leverage of your swing through the ball.

The fairway woods

Throughout this book we have highlighted the reasons some women struggle to achieve distance and we have offered solutions, including properly-fit equipment, course strategy, a good set up, swing fundamentals, and strength training. We now focus on an area of the game that is vital to those who don't hit the ball a long way off the tee—the fairway woods.

One swing for all clubs

A set of golf clubs features a progression of increasing loft coupled with decreasing shaft length, so your driver looks quite different from your sand wedge. Because the clubs are different, many golfers think they need a different swing for each club. Actually you need only one swing regardless of the club you are using. As you learned in Chapter 2 on the set up, your ball position and stance width change for different clubs while your set up and swing are fundamentally the same. Since your woods are longer, you'll be farther away from the ball, but the relationship of your club to your body never changes if you adhere to the principles of good posture.

Without any effort on your part, the look of your swing changes as you progress from long clubs to short ones. For example, since your driver has a long shaft and you are naturally farther from the ball, your swing plane is flatter (more around you). At the other extreme, your short-shafted sand wedge puts you closer to the ball and therefore your swing plane is steeper (more above you). The key is to make a good set up and swing, letting the design of the club dictate the look of your swing.

Good and bad lies

Although you don't make a conscious effort to change your swing, the flatter swing plane of a fairway wood produces a sweeping motion

Regardless of the club that you're using, the fundamentals of your golf swing stay the same.

through the ball. This is a motion that requires a good lie.

▨ The more the ball sits on top of the grass, the more you can sweep it with a long club.

▨ The more the ball sits down in the grass, the more lofted a club you will need to produce a steeper, more descending motion to pluck the ball from this lie.

This is why your driver, the club that produces the greatest sweeping motion, is always used off a tee, which is the perfect lie for sweeping the ball away.

When you are far from the green and the distance dictates a three wood, be sure your lie allows the ball to be swept away. You've always got to play the odds in golf, and the odds are that if you don't have a good lie, then the longer the club you will need the more you are going to mis-hit the ball. And it's always better to hit the shorter club solidly than it is to take the longer club and hit it fat or thin. So make it a rule to use your three wood from a good lie where the ball sits up on top of the grass.

When the ball sits down into the grass, especially in the rough, your five and seven woods are excellent choices. Since their shafts are slightly shorter and your ball position is not as far forward, you'll contact the ball with the descending motion that is necessary to get your ball airborne. However, remember that your motion and the club itself produce the loft; you simply make a good swing without helping the ball into the air.

Note: your lofted fairway woods also feature small heads and, in most cases, specially designed soles which keep the club moving smoothly through the ball if you happen to hit slightly behind it. These same features are effective in the rough since they allow the club to skim through the grass just behind the ball.

Lofted fairway woods are a popular trend in golf. Not only have the 5 and 7 woods replaced the 3 and 4 irons in many golfers' bags but 9 and 11 woods are also gaining popularity among golfers who struggle with their irons.

Both long and short hitters can lower their scores by mastering their fairway woods.

Michelle McGann's distance

Michelle McGann's ability to keep her head behind the ball is a key to her powerful swing but don't confuse this with the over-used advice to keep your head down. You can keep your head down but it doesn't guarantee you'll keep it behind the ball at impact. And it not only goes against the way your body is put together but it is also detrimental to keep your head down much past impact. Focus on keeping your chin pointing behind the ball until your right shoulder pushes it up after the ball is gone. When you allow your head to be drawn up as your shoulders turn through the ball, you can complete your golf swing and finish in balance.

Michelle McGann is one of the longest drivers on the LPGA Tour, hitting a golf ball farther than almost any woman who has ever played the game. What many people don't realize is that she hits the ball farther than the majority of men, even some on the PGA Tour. McGann's physique plays a large part in her distance capabilities. She is tall, with long limbs that produce a wide swing arc, and her body is big, strong and flexible. Although you may never reach Michelle's distances in one shot, you will improve your own distance by learning the keys to her powerful swing.

One clue to her distance can be found in the LPGA Tour's 1996 Player Guide, where working out gets equal ranking with traveling and shopping on her list of favorite things to do. There is no question that her strength contributes to her distance, and our fitness chapter (see page 144) can help you in this area. In fact, Michelle's own personal trainer, Randy Myers, is our expert for your golf fitness program. If you are serious about gaining distance, be sure to follow his advice.

Although Michelle has a great combination of physical strength and size, her swing technique is her greatest asset. Strength and size are useless in golf if you don't know how to use them and Mike Adams, her swing coach, has helped blend all of her physical assets with a swing that maximizes them.

She has a long, low, one-piece takeaway and she sets her leverage, the bending of the wrists and right elbow, rather late in her backswing. These features, together with the benefit of her long arms, create a huge swing arc which is one of the contributing factors to her superior distance.

Takeaway

Although it works well for her, Michelle McGann's takeaway is one you'll want to be careful about copying. Unless you have strong arms and hands, this takeaway causes a woman of average strength more harm than good. In the section on swing mechanics you learned to cock your wrists much earlier in the swing which makes the club head very light since it is literally underneath, and therefore supported by your hands. The later you set your wrists, the heavier the club head becomes as it moves away from your body and works up against gravity. With a late wrist set you run the risk of the club head gaining too much momentum and getting out of control. For golfers who aren't as strong as Michelle, this momentum usually pulls them up out of their golf posture and causes them to lose control of the club at the top of their swing.

Shoulder turn

Michelle McGann's swing also features a big shoulder turn, which is a result of her flexibility. Her shoulders are well behind the ball at the top of her swing and her weight is fully loaded on her right side. It is important to note that although her turn is big and her swing arc is wide and high, her weight never gets outside her right hip or foot.

Tempo and coil

From this position, her excellent tempo keeps the

club on plane as it starts its return to the ball. Her tempo is helped by the fact that she has moved the mass of her body behind the ball in a powerfully coiled position. Swings that don't produce coil are characterized by an abrupt hitting action from the top of the swing that forces the club off plane. Michelle simply allows her coil to unwind into the ball, and her look is one of effortless power.

Head behind ball

Her backswing shoulder turn reverses itself into the ball and her arms extend fully through impact where her legs drive through the ball as she turns her left hip behind her. But, like every accurate power hitter, her head stays fixed behind the ball at impact creating a catapult effect which slings the club through the ball. Considering the force of the forward momentum of her swing, the strength required to hold this position is significant. All else being equal, if Michelle wasn't strong enough to hold this position, the power she generates in her backswing would be far less useful.

Full finish

Michelle's body releases to a truly full finish showing the force of what came before. Her head, chest, and legs face the target and her right foot is turned up on its toe with the majority of her weight on her left side. The most important lesson from her swing is her ability to create coil. In doing so, she uses her strength to hold her body in good posture and balance throughout her swing.

Though she generates an enormous amount of power, Michelle McGann's swing looks smooth and easy. She achieves the look of "effortless power" by combining her natural assets, strength, size, and coordination, with technically sound swing mechanics that begin from a fundamentally solid set up.

Star swings

The stylish Michelle McGann is one of the longest hitters on the LPGA Tour.

I n this chapter you'll get a close-up look at some of the finest players on the LPGA Tour from Hall of Fame member Patty Sheehan to bright new stars like Emilee Klein. Each swing has differences based on the individual's body build, so if you build your own swing based on these models, it's important to pick a player whose body type is similar to your own.

You'll notice that the shorter, more broadly built players, such as Jane Geddes, tend to swing the club a bit shorter at the top of their swings then their more supple counterparts. Very balanced body types, such as Patty Sheehan, swing the club more around them and to the standard position where the club shaft is approximately parallel to the ground at the top of the swing and

their left arm matching their shoulder incline. Long-limbed or tall body types, such as Julie Inkster, tend to swing the club in a longer, more upright arc with their left arm at a greater angle than their shoulders.

There are also swing elements that these players have in common, features all great golfers share. You'll see how they build coil (the amount of shoulder turn versus hip turn), and leverage, the cocking of the wrists, both of which combine to maximize power (see Chapter 3 on swing mechanics). You'll also notice how well they control the club throughout their swings. In a sense,

Chapter four

50

a woman's swing must be more efficient than a man's because they're generally not as big structurally, nor as strong, so by necessity great women players tend to produce swings that are true models of efficiency.

Hall of Fame member Mickey Wright is a good example with one of the finest golf swings of all time, both esthetically and functionally. Wright perfected what has come to be known as the "modern swing," where the big muscles of the body control the small ones, and the power of leverage is maximized. In a misguided effort to gain power, many amateurs lift their arms high above them and minimize the use of bigger muscles in deference to the small muscles of the hands and arms. In doing so, leverage and coil are also minimized. What you'll notice in each of these players is how their swings, some long and flowing, some short and crisp, all operate under the principles of coil and leverage. Implementing these features in your own golf swing will pay you rich rewards on the golf course.

Less upper body strength can be a handicap for some women but an even greater problem can be the fact that most women are very flexible. Flexibility is a problem for some women because it can hinder their ability to build coil in their golf swings. Thus while too little flexibility can be a disadvantage, so can too much. Men generally have less flexibility which, to a point, can be an advantage in golf because, if they know how, men can build coil easily in their swings. The goal for women, especially those with excessive flexibility, is to incorporate both set up and swing fundamentals which moderate their flexibility and enhance coil.

As you examine the swings of these players, you'll see many of them keep their left foot anchored on the ground in their backswings. And those who don't keep it down, let the heel be dragged inward and upward by the motion of their backswings. But none consciously lift the foot, a common swing ailment among amateurs that ruins coil and contributes to the club being mis-routed. When your left foot stays stable, you'll find it easier to turn your upper body more than your lower body during your backswing, the first order of business for creating distance.

As part of creating coil, you'll also see how these players turn their shoulders against their hips and legs. Amateurs who suffer from a lack of distance often turn a lot in their backswings, but the hips and shoulders turn in equal amounts so minimum coil is created. If you're looking to add distance to your golf shots, notice how these professionals keep their lower body rather quiet in relation to the amount their upper body turns during the backswing. Remember, there is a turn in every coil, but not necessarily a coil in every turn. To create maximum force, you should think coil, not turn.

If you're stronger and less flexible than the average woman, you'll still want to pay close attention to these principles of coil and leverage. Golf is one sport where brute force holds little advantage. To do this you'll need to learn how to channel your strength by creating the swing most suitable to your body build. Even strong and powerfully built players like Brandie Burton and Michelle McGann need to satisfy the principles of coil and leverage in a way that best matches their physique to their technique.

Brandie Burton

Brandie Burton began playing golf at the age of nine and throughout her amateur career she collected numerous victories. In addition, she was runner-up at the 1989 US Women's Amateur Championship and qualified for the US Women's Open Championship three times before turning professional. In her year at Arizona State University she was ranked the number one woman collegiate golfer and won six of the seven tournaments on her schedule. Burton turned professional after that year and won Rookie of the Year honors for her eight top ten finishes in 1991. In her third year on Tour, she reached one million dollars in earnings faster than any other player in history and was the LPGA Tour's youngest millionaire ever. That same year she won her first major championship, The du Maurier Ltd. Classic, one of four Tour victories through 1995.

1 Brandie starts her swing from a solid, balanced position. Since she is broadly built and muscular, she flares both feet out at address to facilitate the turn of her body. Both her left and right hand are in a strong grip position and the ball is farther back in her stance than the standard driver position off the left heel.

2 She starts her motion with a gentle cocking of her wrists followed almost immediately by her left arm and chest turning away from the ball as evidenced by the movement of her shirt logo. Notice her lower body is in an identical position to frame one with her hips still square to the target line. This is the beginning of coil, i.e. turning the top of her body more than the bottom. Though a powerful woman, Brandie is already starting to set the club head up with her wrists to make use of the power of leverage.

3 Her lower body shows marked signs of responding to the motion in her upper body. Her right hip has turned back over her right heel, and her left shoulder has begun to move behind the ball. At this point, she's set the club into a fully leveraged position. Although she's turned her back to the target, her hands are still in front of her chest, pushing the club away, adding width to her swing arc. A common error among amateurs is to get their hands well behind them at this point, a difficult position from which to return the club to the ball.

4 Her lower body has completed its turn back as her shoulders deliver the club to the top of her swing. At the completion of Brandie's backswing her lower body has stabilized and her left shoulder has turned against it and behind the ball. Her powerfully coiled position is evident from the creases in the back of her shirt and the tautness of her left sleeve. Brandie gets the club to the standard parallel to the ground position at the top but, because of her body type and flexibility, she can do so only by bending her left elbow at the top of her swing. Some might call this an error but in a swing this powerful, with the club completely in her control, it's more appropriately named an "individual characteristic." The

question is, should you copy it? If you're an elite athlete who practices and plays for a living, and it works for you, then the answer is yes. Otherwise, you'd be wise to concentrate on the more fundamental aspects Brandie beautifully demonstrates.

5 To start her downswing, her right elbow tucks back to her side putting her arms back in front of her body. From the top of her swing she shifted her weight into her left hip and she now begins to turn it powerfully behind her, a move that delivers the club directly to the ball. Though her left hip is turning away from the ball, her head and neck have stayed in their position behind it, creating a reversal of the coil she built in her backswing.

6 At impact she continues the rotation of her body to bring the club to the ball. Though her arms are following the rotation, her head and neck are still firmly planted behind the ball. Here she demonstrates a position common to a good player, but uncommon to a poor player: her left arm, hand, and club shaft are in line with the lower right leg, which shows she's allowed her right side to release. Also, notice her right heel is working to the inside rather than up. When amateurs let their right heel "flip out" toward the target line before impact, it causes their club to cut across the ball. The right foot working in allows the club to be delivered more from the inside so it comes to the ball along the target line rather than across it.

7 Brandie's arms swing past her, literally dragging her up toward her finish position. She's fully released the leverage she built in her backswing as is evident from the recocking of her wrists on her throughswing.

8 Brandie's finish is a result of her right knee "getting friendly" with her left. From the top of her swing to her finish, her left knee was moving away from the right which was chasing it. At the completion of her swing, her ankle, knee, hip, and shoulder joint are stacked one on top of the other, indicating that she has rotated her powerful body fully through the ball.

Jane Geddes

1 Jane is similar in body type to Brandie Burton so their swings have many similarities. At address, her arms hang comfortably from her shoulders with her left arm and the club shaft forming a straight line down to the ball. Her hands are in a strong position, rotated to the right of the center of the shaft, with the ball positioned slightly back. She's bent to the ball from her hips, shown by the fact that her knees are relaxed but not excessively flexed. Her feet are slightly flared.

2 As Jane starts back, her shoulders turn and her hands push the club away from her chest, an action that begins to pull her behind the golf ball. With her left foot and lower leg serving as resistance, she's already begun to build coil, evident by the creases in her shirt. Though the motion is minimal, she's in the process of loading her weight into her right side but only in response to the motion of her upper body.

3 Before reaching the top of her swing, Jane has set the club into a full leverage position. Her hands are relatively low and the club head is high. Good players elevate the club by setting the wrists and turning the shoulders rather than just lifting their arms. Over-lifting your arms curtails your ability to rotate your body correctly. The correct rotation is evident here as Jane's right hip has turned over her right heel and her left shoulder has rotated behind the ball.

4 At the top of her swing, Jane's left foot has rolled onto its inner rim in response to the pull of her upper body turn, but it hasn't lifted. A common mistake is to let your left knee get too close to your right at the top of your swing, but Jane keeps the distance between her knees the same as it was at address to preserve her excellent coil. Her shoulders have turned well past her hips and the club is completely under

control at the top of her swing, two of the main reasons why she is one of the longest hitters on Tour.

5 On the downswing, the pressure of her weight moves over her left heel, and her right arm tucks into her right side, the combination of which puts her arms back in front of her body. Every good player gets their arms back in front of their body at impact so they can deliver the club to the ball with the full force of their body.

6 At the top of her swing (frame 4), Jane's left shoulder was directly under her chin, but as she starts her drive back to the ball, that shoulder moves forward and upward, a key move that drops her right arm back to her side. At this point many amateurs let their right shoulder move out toward the target line from the top of their swing, an error known as "over the top," causing weak shots that slice to the right. In order to approach the ball on the correct path, it is of critical importance to start the upper body portion of your downswing by lowering the right shoulder and raising the left.

7 Jane has beautiful extension after impact, the only time in the golf swing both arms are straight. The club has fully released and still her head is well back and just starting to be pulled up. Good players look under the ball as it leaves and they do so because their head is behind the ball through impact. Then, as the momentum of their arm swing begins to pull them up, their head swivels with their eyes looking under the ball.

8 Jane's follow through is classic. Her head, chest, and hips face her target, and her back foot serves as a rudder. Notice there are no wrinkles in her right shoe, indicating all of her weight has completely transferred to her left side.

Jane Geddes **continued**

In her 13 years as a professional, Jane Geddes has consistently ranked as one of the longest drivers of the ball on Tour. In 1995, she averaged 252.4 yards, which is farther than some men on the PGA Tour. Standing only five feet five inches, she produces her distance with an incredibly efficient swing. We have included a down-the-target line sequence of her swing because it is a perfect model for maximum use of leverage and coil.

1 Jane hovers her driver above the ground at address, as did the legendary Jack Nicklaus who, in his day, was also a power hitter. For some players, hovering the club in this manner allows them a greater awareness of the weight of the club head and induces relaxation in their arms and shoulders at address. If you find you're very tense over the ball, you might give this method a try.

2 As Jane takes the club away, notice how the big muscles of her body have caused the club to move. Though her hands have moved back they are still very low, down by her thighs where they started, indicating that she has not lifted the club in any way. Unlike her hands, the club head has traveled a good distance from its position at address, but it has been swung to this position, gaining additional ground through her wrists which are beginning to cock the club head up. Her lower body is showing subtle signs of responding but there is no overt action. By minimizing early lower body movement, she prevents the club from getting too far behind her body and starts to create coil early in her swing.

3 From here she'll continue the combined motion of arm swing, shoulder turn, and wrist cock to elevate the club to the top. Her lower body has moved in sympathy with her big shoulder turn behind the ball. Her weight is fully loaded onto her right leg, solidly contained on the inner rim of her right foot which is a key to her power. Jane has established her right leg as a post around which she's turning. Her elbows and hands form a triangle at the top, the base of which is level to the ground. Had she exaggerated her hip turn or whipped the club in behind her with her hands, you'd see the right elbow much lower than the left, a difficult error that causes the body to race out in front of the arms through impact.

4 The most important element to observe in Jane's downswing is that the club, specifically the grip end,

is traveling down, not around. The club has moved a much greater distance relative to the movement of her body and that's appropriate since it has a much greater distance to travel to impact. You can see that Jane has transferred the pressure of her weight to her left side, which helps drop the club downward; from here she can begin her powerful hip rotation to deliver the club around to the ball.

5 Just a fraction of a second before impact, her left hip has turned well behind her and is pulling her right side into the ball. Most importantly, the club is back to the ball with the shaft on the same angle it established at address.

6 Since the club head is moving at such a high rate of speed it appears as a blur in the frame. Note though how the blur of the club head is directly in front of her chest, indicating that she's used the full force of her powerful body to deliver the club to the ball. Her shoulders are rotating beautifully around the inclined axis of her spine, a reversal of the path they transcribed in the backswing. Often amateurs have difficulty with their swings because they straighten their spine and cause their shoulders to turn too level to the ground. Make a slow-motion swing in a mirror and check that your shoulders turn as Jane's do, but any change in your posture during the critical parts of your swing will disrupt your shoulder plane.

7 Jane is gracefully drawn up and out of her impact position as a natural result of the club swinging past her. Her wrists are recocking on the throughswing in response to the unleashing of leverage through the ball.

8 Jane's finish is full and excellent, a complete representation and response to all that came before—a swing that is fundamentally a power house of efficiency.

Emilee Klein

In her first year on Tour, Emilee Klein won more money than any other rookie in 1995 and posted two second-place finishes, an appropriate transition from her sensational amateur career. She was the 1988 California Amateur Champion, the 1991 American Junior Golf Association Player of the Year, and was an AJGA First Team All American for four consecutive years. Her other victories included the 1991 US Junior Girls Championship, the 1993 Broadmoor, the 1993 North/South Amateur, and 1993 Amateur of the Year award. During her two-year tenure at Arizona State University she earned All-American status both years, was the 1994 NCAA Champion, and the 1994 Collegiate Player of the Year. In 1996, Emilee got her first two professional victories, including a British Open title, and she finished the year among the top 10 money winners.

Emilee has a unique swing due to her unusual set up position which features a very erect posture. But while it looks unusual, the analysis will show her swing adheres to the basic principles of coil and leverage.

1 Emilee is a very accurate player because, due to her set up, she doesn't have a lot of wasted body motion. Neither foot is flared and her knees are pinched in, both of which minimize lower body movement. The back of her left hand faces the target as does the palm of her right hand, a configuration known as a relatively weak grip. Her hands are set in the mid-line of her body, encouraging the more rounded swing arc that is her trademark.

2 Emilee's erect posture causes her to swing the club well away from her and then around her in her back-swing with minimal hip turn. In fact, her lower body is so quiet that she appears to have a reverse weight shift, but, by frame 4, you'll see she's well coiled into her right side. She is young and very flexible in her shoulder joints, a condition allowing her maximum arm swing and minimal leg action. This flexibility is only an asset if you can find a way not to over-turn your hips and legs, a problem Emilee has solved nicely with her set up.

3 Emilee has set the leverage for her golf swing, though she does so somewhat later than most players. Her right knee has straightened (though it hasn't locked) and serves as a buttress to receive the transfer of weight so important to her coil. Her left heel has begun to pull off the ground but only in response to her upper body turning behind the ball. In a swing that is known more for its accuracy than its power, perhaps Emilee could benefit by keeping her left heel down to add a bit more coil.

4 Emilee's weight is fully loaded on her right side. Though her left heel has come off the ground, the position of her left knee shows the heel has moved more in than up, a further indication her weight has transferred fully to her right side. True error occurs when amateurs lift their heel up and the left knee juts out toward the target line, indicating their weight has remained on their left side.

5 Coming down, Emilee's hips turn marginally as her right shoulder drops and her left shoulder raises, a move that allows her to swing the club directly to the ball without cutting across it. Through impact her legs act as stabilizers and she gains power by hitting across a braced left leg. Since her left leg is already straight and her right leg is almost straight, she's generating a lot of her force through arm swing and the release of the leverage in her wrists.

6 A further indication of her dominating arm swing is that her shoulders are in virtually the same position in frames 5 and 6, showing a strong hand and arm release. With a weak grip she must have a hand and arm release in order to square the club face. Like all good players, her head is behind the ball through impact and her left hip is moving behind her rather than toward the target.

7 As Emilee swings through, her arms reach maximum extension and then begin to pull her body up into her follow through. Her right forearm has rotated well over her left, further evidence that her swing is geared toward a hand and arm release rather than a body release.

8 The creases in her right shoe indicate that Emilee's follow through is less than full because she doesn't use all of the weight of her body to hit the ball. She is primarily an arms and hands player, which is fine as long as the basics of leverage and coil are satisfied. Emilee has built her golf swing and game around pinpoint accuracy and incredible touch.

Julie Inkster

Star *profile*

Though Julie Inkster is hardly as well known as Tiger Woods, her career began in a similar fashion after she won three consecutive US Amateur Titles. A four-time All-American during her years at San Jose State University, she joined the LPGA Tour in 1983 and captured her first victory in just her fifth event. Julie received Rookie of the Year honors, winning two major championships, the first rookie to accomplish such a feat. Her best year was 1986 when she won four times and posted her career low round of 64 on two occasions. In 1990, she gave birth to her first child and played a limited schedule, but in her next two years on Tour she won twice and earned over half a million dollars. In 1994, her second daughter was born, but she still managed eight top 20 finishes, and second place in a limited schedule. Her phenomenal career is highlighted by three major championships and a total of 15 victories in 13 years on the LPGA Tour.

1 Julie addresses the ball with a neutral grip and excellent posture. She plays the ball a little further back in her stance than most players. Unlike Emilee Klein, her feet are flared out with her knees pointing in the same direction as her toes, giving her a solid foundation for her upright swing arc.

2 Like many long-limbed golfers, Julie's takeaway is a one-piece action, with her shoulders, arms, hands, and club all working back and away from her body as a unit rather then around and behind her. In contrast to Brandie Burton and Patty Sheehan, she doesn't fully set the club until she's near the top of her backswing. While there is a lot of arm swing it all occurs as part of coil. Julie does not "pick the club up." She "coils it up" and this is an important distinction.

3 Her lower body has turned away from the target in response to the movement of her long, one-piece takeaway but she hasn't allowed this action to cause her hips to sway, a problem for some amateurs who employ this style (right hip slides laterally outside the right leg instead of turning over the right heel). Julie's lower body has finished its backswing motion and will remain in this position while her upper body continues to turn against it, cranking up her coil. Like many players of this body type, she sets the club very late in her swing, between frames 3 and 4. The danger for golfers who don't have strong arms and hands is that a late set leaves the club in a heavy position because the club head is not underneath the supporting pedestal of the hands. But Julie is strong so she manages her late set beautifully and she keeps the club head in complete control.

4 Though her turn is full, her left foot is firmly planted. Her downswing is initiated by a shifting of her weight from the heel of her right foot to the ball of her left foot, a move that is assisted by the late set of the club. This motion drops her hands and arms down before they come around to the ball.

5 Once the left leg has accepted her weight and her arms have dropped into position, she begins a powerful hip rotation through the ball. Her left hip is turning behind her even though her right knee is driving toward the ball. Also, her right foot is off the ground very early, which is characteristic of players who swing the club in a high arc and approach the ball from a steep angle. She lets her right heel be pulled off the ground in response to the momentum of her swing. Some amateurs push off their right foot which causes a lot of thin shots.

6 Julie fully releases the leverage in her wrists and slings the club past her neck, which is in a rock solid position behind the ball. Throughout her swing, she turns her shoulders perfectly around the axis of her inclined spine. They come level to the ground only after her spine straightens at the finish of her swing.

7 Julie has marvelous extension here with her arms still straight, a result of the velocity of the club moving down the target line. And it is this velocity that pulls her up into her follow through position.

8 Her arms swing through and she finishes in a very upright position with her hands and arms over her shoulders. A beautiful golf swing.

Patty Sheehan

Star *profile*

The LPGA Hall of Fame is commonly considered the most difficult achievement in all of sports and only 14 professionals have been able to fulfill its elite entry requirements. Early in 1993, Patty Sheehan reached this lofty goal by winning her thirtieth tournament, and added a fourth major championship to her credit later that year. After an impressive amateur career highlighted by her victory at the 1980 AIAW National Championship, she joined the Tour that same year. She claimed her first victory in 1981 and has won at least once every year since, the only exception being 1987 when she lost a major championship playoff to Betsy King. In 1983 and 1984 she won four tournaments, bettering that achievement in 1990 with five victories and over $700,000 in earnings. Through 1995 Patty won 34 LPGA tournaments, including five major championships plus a Women's British Open title. In 1996 Patty captured her sixth major championship victory of her career, the Nabisco Dinah Shore.

1 Patty's set up features a strong left hand grip, both her feet are flared, and her knees point in the direction of her toes. Her spine is tilted a tad to the right which sets her behind the ball before she even starts her swing. Her arms hang directly downward from her shoulders, indicating that she's bent to the ball from her hips with no hunching of her back. Her left arm is on top of her chest, facilitating an unobstructed arm swing across her chest.

2 In a style typical of the "modern swing," one well suited to Patty's balanced body type, she starts the club back by swinging her left arm across her chest with an early fold of her right elbow and an early set of her wrists. At this point her weight hasn't completely moved to her right heel but it is in the process of doing so.

3 Here her right hip begins to turn over her right heel, and her left knee begins to be pulled behind the ball. She's already created a tremendous amount of coil and she'll increase it as her lower body begins to stabilize and her shoulders and arms continue to turn with her swing.

4 At the top of her backswing, Patty's left arm is swung fully across her chest and has coiled her shoulders behind the ball. Her left foot has been dragged off the ground late in her backswing.

5 Here you can see why Patty has achieved such greatness in her career. She holds her leveraged position, the angle of power, longer than almost anyone who has played the game. The club head is still behind and above her right shoulder but her arms are back in front of her chest and her hands are almost at impact, a fully leveraged position which is reminiscent of Mickey Wright and Ben Hogan. She accomplishes this because her right side holds its position as her left side turns behind her and pulls her arms down. To further assist her in this much sought after position, her left shoulder has moved out from under, and, most importantly, up from under her chin.

6 Notice the triangle formed by her chest and forearms with the shaft of the club bisecting it, an indication of a full and perfectly timed release of her arms, wrists and right side. The beauty of it is that her swing center, located just below her throat, is behind the ball as she delivers her club head, a prerequisite for solid, powerful contact. You can see the force of this momentum continue well into her follow through as the club wraps around her body in frame 8.

7 Patty continues to rotate through the ball with her lower body. She maintains her spine angle for a long time and hangs back just a little bit as both arms extend through the shot. Her left leg is still slightly flexed because she still hasn't fully rotated her hips.

8 She finishes in a perfect follow through position. You'll notice a slight wrinkling in her right shoe, indicating it's holding some weight, but since her follow through is so long and full, this is a recoil from what was a complete release to her left side. Patty's swing would easily qualify for the Golf Swing Hall of Fame, if there was such a thing.

Chip — a low running shot played from about 5 yds from the green

Pitch — a lofted shot played from an area around the green

Caroline Pierce

Caroline Pierce's competitive skill began to show when she reached the semi-final round of the 1979 English Girls Championship and flourished in 1980 and 1981 when she was an English Girls International Champion. At Houston Baptist University, she continued her winning ways earning All-American honors in 1983 and 1984. After a slow start on the LPGA Tour, she began to build momentum in 1994 with some top ten finishes and almost $85,000 in earnings. She more than doubled her earnings in 1995 with several more top ten finishes and a second place finish at The JAL Big Apple Classic. Caroline earned her first Tour victory here the following year and did so in style. She was the only player in the field to finish under par, winning with a five stroke advantage over a field of top players. She finished 1996 ranked twenty-second in earnings and continues to leapfrog over her prior personal bests. Both Emilee Klein and Caroline Pierce stand about five feet five inches tall, with long limbs and slim bodies, so it is no surprise that their swings look similar.

1 Caroline addresses the ball with rather erect posture, which causes her shoulders to turn more level to the ground. The ball is off her left heel, perfectly positioned for a driver. This excellent ball position encourages her square address position, i.e. shoulders, hips, and feet all parallel to her target line, a strong element in her accuracy. Her arms hang comfortably with no hint of tension. Her left foot is flared out at address which helps her build coil as she turns away from the ball, a good idea since her body is the type that turns easily but has difficulty creating coil.

2 If you have a thin frame like Caroline's, you'll need to guard against taking the club too far inside on your takeaway. Her erect posture serves to keeps, her hands moving as they should, back down the line of her toes rather than in behind her as is evident from the fact that her hands and the shaft of the club are still in front of her chest. Her takeaway is a one-piece motion with a very late set of her wrists, the weight of which she controls perfectly in frame 3.

3 The function of Caroline's backswing is to get the mass of her body behind the ball. It is not very long nor does she create maximum coil since her hips have turned almost as much as her shoulders. Though her backswing is short, her hands are in an upright position as a result of her one-piece takeaway.

4 To start her downswing, her hips make a subtle move laterally toward the target while her shoulders remain in a very closed position pointing to the right of target. At this late point in her swing you now see an increase in the tension between upper and lower body,

satisfying her need for coil. It's most important to note that, though her hips move toward the target to start her downswing, her head and neck have held their position behind the ball, a prerequisite for powerful contact because it's another element of coil. As she reverses the direction of her club she drops her arms back down, in the complete absence of any hitting impulse by her hands.

5 Once the lateral move of her hips is completed and her weight has transferred to her left leg, she begins to turn her left hip behind her. Caroline's arms, having dropped the club down into a perfect position, are now ready to deliver the club head to the ball.

6 She looks very stable here with her right foot remaining low to the ground. She's hitting against a firm left side, exhibiting the classic impact position of all good players with the back of her left hand facing the target and the club shaft in line with her left arm.

7 Late into her follow through she still has the club shaft pointing at her chest with her elbows in front of her, a sign that she has fully released her right side including her right shoulder. Note how the toe of her left shoe is turned up a tad, showing that her weight is perfectly distributed, starting from the ball of her foot back to her left heel.

8 An elegant finish with her weight fully posted on her left side and the club shaft across her neck. It shows she has held nothing back yet is in complete control. A good finish looks like the player could stay in that pose for a long time and certainly the comfortable and relaxed Caroline sets an excellent example.

Michelle McGann

Having joined the LPGA Tour at 18 years old, Michelle McGann's amateur career was brief but impressive: three times Florida State Junior Champion, the 1987 USGA Junior Girls Champion, and also the American Junior Golf Associations Rolex Junior Player of the Year. As a teenager, she got off to a somewhat slow start in her first two years on tour, but in 1991 she earned over $120,000 and hasn't looked back. Michelle has steadily increased her earnings and scoring average through the 1990's and got her first two wins in 1995. Setting yet a higher standard in 1996 she won three times and earned almost $500,000. Michelle is one of the longest drivers on Tour, averaging just over 255 yards per drive in 1996. A student of Mike Adams, she is poised to have a long and impressive career on the LPGA Tour.

1 With the exception of the putting stroke and the modified swings for other short game shots, your full swing is the same whether you're hitting a full wedge or a driver. In Chapter 4, you learned some keys to Michelle's distance with a driver. In this sequence she is hitting her wedge with a full swing. Though her posture and ball position change to accommodate the club's specifications, you'll see her swing is basically the same.

Since she's hitting a very lofted club, she plays the ball back in her stance to account for the club's more vertical descent. In addition, her stance is narrow with her heels under her hips and she's bent to the ball more because of the short-shafted club.

Michelle's body features give her a natural advantage. She's tall, with a broad muscular frame and plenty of flexibility. Her swing features a big turn and a wide high swing arc but since she's very flexible she addresses the ball with her feet very straight. Less flexible players flare their toes out to facilitate the turn of their bodies back and through, but Michelle encourages her body to build coil by limiting her flexibility with the position of her feet.

2 The hallmark of Michelle's swing is a one-piece take-away, meaning her chest, arms, club shaft, and club head all move away from the ball as one unit. In contrast to Patty Sheehan who sets the club head up very early, Michelle keeps the club head low to create a huge swing arc, a key to her power. There are various ways to take the club away but, like all great players, Michelle's lower body motion at this point in her swing is a subtle reaction to the motion in her upper body

3 Late in her backswing Michelle has fully set her wrists as you can see from the 90-degree angle formed by the club shaft and her forearm. With her hands high above her, her leverage fully set and her left shoulder well coiled behind the ball, she is in a powerful position to hit the ball.

She's not as tightly coiled as some of the other players but you'll see that she increases her coil in the downswing.

4 Most of the keys to Michelle's power can be seen in this frame. Here she increases coil because her shoulders remain turned away from the target but her hips have begun their downswing turn in the opposite direction. Also, just a milli-second before impact, she still has the club in a fully leveraged position, i.e. the 90-degree angle between the shaft and forearms is identical to that in frame 4. Her feet are firmly planted on the ground, where they've been throughout her swing and where they'll stay until just after impact.

5 With her arms back in front of her chest she now begins to release the leverage of her golf swing into the ball in conjunction with the late uncoiling of her shoulders.

6 At the precise moment of impact, Michelle masterfully returns the club and her body to the position they held at address. Except for the dynamic effects of motion and her left hip turning aggressively behind her, this picture is almost identical to frame 1.

7 Just past impact you can see how her head is behind the ball and will be drawn up by the turn of her body. Both of her arms have fully extended as she unwinds her body through the ball. Again you see almost a duplicate of the corresponding backswing photo (frame 2) indicating Michelle swung her club in a circle and hasn't created any odd angles by lunging or lurching. Hers is an effortless power that comes from the proper use of her natural assets channeled through a technically sound and powerful golf swing.

8 Her finish is perfect—a full, yet smooth, release of her club and body through the golf ball.

Barb Thomas

In 1995, Barb Thomas had her best year ever on the LPGA Tour, winning the Hawaiian Ladies Open and posting five top 20 finishes. Early in her amateur career she was the Iowa Junior champion in both 1978 and 1979. From there she went on to an impressive collegiate record at Tulsa University where she earned All-American honors in 1980 and posted a convincing third-place finish in the 1982 NCAA Championships. She qualified for the LPGA Tour in her first attempt by holing out a bunker shot on the final hole of the tournament. Barb has improved her golf swing consistently throughout her career and offers a fine example of strong golf technique.

1 Barb is a very straight driver of the ball due to her excellent set up. The golf ball is perfectly positioned off her left heel and her left arm hangs comfortably atop her chest ready to swing freely. Her feet are straight at address which will serve to increase her coil back and through her golf swing.

2 Barb's arms swing back, creating stretch in her left side, the initial element of her coil. Notice as her arms swing, her shoulders have moved only slightly to accommodate the arm swing and her lower body has maintained its address position. Each of these features adds to her early development of coil.

3 Now her right hip has turned over her right heel, establishing the right side pivot point which will serve as the lower body axis for her backswing. Her left shoulder has turned as it should, around her inclined spine and therefore appears to move downward. Though her arms are still over an extension of her toe line, her wrists have set the club head into a fully leveraged position. In doing so, her hands serve as a pedestal for the weight of the club head as it is elevated to the top of her swing. These are the takeaway characteristics of the modern, body controlled golf swing.

4 At the top of her swing, both feet are planted firmly on the ground. Barb's knees haven't moved much, yet her upper body has fully rotated as shown by the fact that her left shoulder is well behind the ball. To create coil in the modern swing three areas need attention: the shoulders and chest (upper body) turn the most; the hips (middle body) turn the next greatest amount; and the knees (lower body) turn the least. Each level produces opposition, and creating the proper ratios between each produces maximum coil. Should any of these levels turn too much the coil would be reduced and so would the potential for power.

5 Here Barb beautifully illustrates the initial movements that deliver the club back to the ball. You can see how much the club is moving down and therefore why it's called a "downswing." To do this, her left hip has turned over her left heel, yet her right side has held its position to maintain her coil. As a result her hands move downward and away from her right shoulder. Called separation, this downward movement of the hands away from the shoulder slots the club, putting it in a perfect position to take advantage of her shoulder and hip rotation which is about to occur. Now her turn works to her benefit to deliver the club to the ball. Had she turned first and left the club up high, she'd need to struggle near impact to get the club down to the ball and to do so she'd have to stop the powerful rotation of her body.

6 Barb has arrived at impact with her lower body leading the way, but notice how her left hip is turning behind her rather than sliding toward the target. Though her weight shifted laterally from frames 4 to 5, from there she began a powerful rotation of her left hip behind her. A common error among amateurs is to continue the lateral motion and neglect the rotational motion. This puts the body well ahead of the ball at impact and greatly diminishes distance potential. As with all players of her caliber, she arrives at impact with the club back in front of her body, and her left arm firmly planted against her chest to add the power of her body to the hit.

7 With the ball well on its way, this frame shows how well Barb has released her leverage and coil into the shot.

8 Her follow through shows she has delivered her energy to the ball efficiently. Her hips are fully turned, her chest faces left of the target, and she is perfectly balanced on her left foot.

Alice Miller

Alice Miller has had a prestigious career both on and off the golf course. She was president of the LPGA Tour in 1993 and that year also received the Powell Award, given annually to a player selected by her peers for her elite level of sportsmanship. At Arizona State University, she played on the 1975 NCAA Championship Team. In 1983 she recorded her first win on tour and has a total of eight LPGA victories thus far. She won four tournaments in 1985, including her first major championship at the Nabisco Dinah Shore, and finished third on the money list. She was the 1991 Bounceback Player of the Year with a victory at the Toledo Classic. Overall she has earned over $1,000,000 on the LPGA Tour.

1 To accommodate her tall, lean frame, Alice stands more upright at address. Her feet are flared out which encourages her hips to turn more. As her swing progresses you'll see how well this matches with her wide high swing arc. She employs a strong grip and matches this perfectly with a ball position that is slightly back of the standard.

2 She starts the club away by letting her left arm swing across her chest. Though her hips have turned somewhat early in her swing she avoids the error of letting this early hip movement drag the club in behind her. The club has transcribed a wide low arc and has arrived at waist high in an unleveraged position. A strong woman, Alice controls the club well at this point, and as her swing continues she avoids any temptation to lift the club to the top, a common error from this position.

3 Her big hip turn has dragged her left heel slightly inward, but her flexible upper body will make a huge turn behind the ball to achieve the proper ratio between upper, middle, and lower body. As she begins to set the leverage for her swing notice the how far the club head has traveled between frames 2 and 3 in relationship to how little her hands have moved. This indicates that her wrists are providing the elevation.

4 At the top, Alice's upper body is well coiled against her hips, and her feet and legs have stabilized to provide a solid platform. She has rolled to the inside rim of her left foot without raising it off the ground—another indication of coil. Her late wrist set has caused a long swing but it matches perfectly with her big hip turn. With her hips turned this far, she's given herself time to start her downswing before her left hip begins turning behind her. Think of your swing as a race to the finish line (impact) where your hands and arms must travel a long way from the top of your swing but your hip journey is much shorter. You want everything to arrive together and you must carefully adjust the elements of your swing in order to achieve synchronization.

5 The transition from backswing to downswing is a segment of the swing where many golfers go wrong. In a good golf swing there are some moves that occur simultaneously and others that are sequential. Starting down there can be no confusion: the left hip must clear while, at the same time, the club drops straight down toward the ground. When done together they preserve Alice's coil; if they occur separately, coil is released and power leaks away. By allowing the club to drop down Alice retains the 90-degree angle created by her left forearm and the club shaft.

6 Just prior to impact, she unplugs her right heel from the ground, which balances the movement of her head down to the ball. You'll notice other players who swing the club on an upright arc, like Julie Inkster and Emilee Klein, perform these complementary moves through impact. Their swings have an "up and down" look and the players who swing the club in a more rotary fashion, such as Patty Sheehan and Jane Geddes, look far more flat-footed just prior to impact. So what would be an error for some is not for others and having a teacher who can distinguish between the two can minimize the time you spend matching the elements of your swing.

7 Like all great players, Alice holds her head firmly in place behind the ball so the club can sling by her with maximum velocity. Her head is dragged up naturally as the force of her motion continues through the ball.

8 On her way to a full finish you can see how her hands are a mirror image of the position they were in at the top of her swing, indicating that she's fully released the club head into and through the ball. To do so efficiently, she's also fully released the power of her body in a proper rotation through the ball as she demonstrates with her excellent finish position.

Chapter five

Putting

One of golf's more frustrating features is the equitable value given to each shot, regardless of the distance required to execute that shot. On your score card, a powerful drive that lands in the center of the fairway is equal to a one-inch putt. But for your total score, putting is the

Though most golfers concentrate on improving their full swings, putting can account for over 40 percent of your score.

skill most heavily weighted since it accounts for about 40 percent of the strokes in an average round of golf. The good news is that putting can save you when your full swing lets you down or your opponent out-distances you off the tee.

Learn to be a good putter

Despite its importance, golfers are famous for neglecting their putting practice in favor of hitting full shots on the driving range. There's no question that power and accuracy in your full swing make you a better player but the easiest and fastest way to lower your handicap is to improve your short game, especially putting. Golfers tend to neglect putting because of a common misconception that good putters are born, not made; in other words—you can't learn to putt. Not true. Good putting can be taught and it's one of the easiest skills to learn. Like any skill it requires practice but with the proper technique, you'll acquire your feel more quickly and keep it a lot longer.

The pendulum is best

Although there are many putting styles, the most natural and dependable is the pendulum motion where your arms, shoulders, and putter act in unison around the fixed axis of your spine. By visualizing the pendulum of a grandfather clock, for example, you'll get a clear idea of its features. The pendulum moves back and forth an equal distance at an even tempo. It stays on a prescribed path, moving neither inside nor outside, because of its fixed axis and the absence of any manipulation. No one is trying to make it go anywhere; it just swings. The same features are desirable in putting: an even tempo and a non-manipulated stroke that remains on a fixed path both back and through the ball. By learning a few fundamentals, you'll experience the simplicity of this motion and enjoy the positive results it produces on the putting green.

The set up

Since golf requires both the powerful movements of a full swing and a delicate touch around and on the green, you'll need two distinctly different motions that cover all aspects of your game, a swing motion and a stroke motion. The swing motion is lower-body oriented with plenty of wrist action, which, when blended correctly, produces long, powerful shots.

The stroke, or pendulum motion, is upper-body oriented without any wrist action, ideal for the precision and short distances required for putting and chipping. Therefore, in the stroke motion you grip the club in a way that quiets your wrists, and which is quite different from your full swing grip where you want maximum wrist cock.

Your putting grip

- Place the left side of the grip against the lifeline of your left hand so that the shaft forms a relatively straight line with your left forearm.

1 Place the side of the putter grip diagonally through the palm of your hand.

2 Place the palm of your right hand against the side of the grip with the thumbs on top of the grip.

The set up *continued*

■ In the same manner, apply your right hand just beneath your left hand, against the right side of the shaft of the putter.

■ Wrap your fingers underneath so they are comfortable and rest your thumbs on the top side of the putter grip. You'll find that the back of your left hand, the palm of your right hand, and the putter face all point in the same direction. To roll the ball accurately with no wrist action, keep these relationships consistent throughout your stroke.

Posture and aiming

1 Once you've set your hands on your putter correctly, take your putting posture by bending

Proper putting posture is created by positioning your eyes directly over the ball. This allows your arms to hang comfortably from your shoulders and encourages a pendulum motion.

forward from your hips until your eyes are directly over the ball so that when you rotate your head to look at the hole, your eyes are looking directly down the target line—just as you would want them to do in any other target game.

2 As with your full swing, remember to first aim your putter down your target line and then align your body square to your target line, giving special attention to your shoulders. Your arms naturally follow the line of your shoulders, and when they are closed at address (your shoulders pointing to the right of the target), your putter head swings on an inside-to-out path that results in a putt pushed to the right. When your shoulders are open at address, your path is outside-to-in and the ball rolls to the left of target. Ideally, in the correct stroke, your putter moves along the target line as long as possible, both back and through the ball.

3 As with your shoulders, position your feet square to your target line so that your arms and hands hang comfortably beneath your shoulders. Your stance is hip width with about 60 percent of your weight kept solidly on your left side as you putt.

4 Keeping your eyes over the ball, flex your knees until your weight is on your heels. It's a good idea to pinch your knees toward each other to guard against any lower body movement during your putting stroke. Remember, a major difference between a stroke for accuracy and a swing for distance is the absence of lower body action. Your lower body should remain stock still as too many moving parts spoil accuracy.

The putting stroke

Your stroke utilizes the top of your spine as the anchor point around which your shoulders rock in an up-and-down motion. This point remains stationary allowing the triangle formed by your shoulders and arms to move like a see-saw or teeter-totter. The triangle must maintain its shape throughout the stroke, with the distance between the elbows constant, which insures the bottom of the putting arc also remains constant.

In a good putting stroke, your shoulders work up and down like a teeter-totter or a see-saw, a motion that keeps the face of your putter square to the target line for as long as possible. If your shoulders work around behind you, your putter face opens and closes throughout your stroke.

The putting stroke *continued*

The pendulum stroke

The pendulum stroke is easier to judge. There has been a good deal said about accelerating the putter head through impact. While it's true that your club head is moving faster at the lowest point of its arc due to gravity, if you try to add speed to your putter, the club face tends to open.

The opposite happens when you force yourself to make a long and stylish back stroke. The odds are that you'll overdo it and swing back too long, forcing you to slow down your putter as it approaches the ball, which has a tendency to shut the club face.

The best way to putt is to forget about trying to manipulate the putter and simply let the principles of the pendulum putting stroke work for you. With the correct pendulum motion there is no conscious "hit" yet your club face is accelerating at impact with the face square to the target line. If you let the image of the pendulum be in control, where the arc on one side of the low point is equal to the arc on the other, your putting stroke naturally finds the correct length and force.

With a proper set up and stroke you'll roll the

ball straight along your target line but since putting greens are sloped and your distance always varies, you'll need to know how to read the greens and vary your speed

The wrist flip is a common error in putting and causes problems with distance control. Poor distance control results in "three putts" which make golf scores skyrocket.

Reading the greens

Putting greens feature contours and slopes that cause your ball to roll at different speeds and in different directions, depending on the position of your ball in relation to the hole. To be a good putter, you'll need to calculate the slope's effect on the speed and direction of your ball.

Obviously when you are at the top of a slope, your ball will roll down the hill with less effort than if you were putting uphill. If you are putting across a slope, your ball will start straight and then fall to the low side of the slope and you'll have to hit it harder because part of its journey is uphill. Figuring out the amount of influence the slope has on your ball and then being able to allow for it in your stroke, is the challenge of putting. Research shows that most golfers don't read enough break into the putt and this affects the

speed of their putt and also its direction. When you read too little break into the putt, you either miss on the high side of the cup because you have to hit the ball hard to hold the line, or you miss it on the low side because you've hit it too softly.

Evaluating a slope

The best way to evaluate the severity of a slope is to position yourself below the hole and look up the hill. For example, when you look up at a

Reading the greens *continued*

Putting greens are treated with great respect by experienced golfers, and beginners can find themselves befuddled by the many customs that take place here. If you're new to golf, here are a few tips that will make you more at home on the putting green.

■ If your golf shoes have spikes, lift your feet when you walk. Dragging them causes cuts and "spike marks" that damage the surface of the green.

■ On your way to your ball, don't walk through the line of another golfer's putt. The "line of the putt" extends not only from their golf ball to the hole, but just past the hole as well.

■ The person furthest from the hole is the first to putt. The person closest to the hole is usually responsible for tending the flagstick or removing it. She should ask the other members of the group if they'd like it tended, or remove it and lay it down in a place where it won't interfere with play.

Learning how to read a green can lower your scores dramatically.

mountain, the severity of its slope is clear, but when you're on top of the mountain looking down, your perception of the slope is not as accurate; it looks much less severe. So to read the green's slope, especially the more subtle contours, take a walk around the hole.

1   You want to see if your putt is uphill or downhill. If you have an uphill putt, you'll get the clearest view of the slope from behind your ball looking back up the hill to the hole. If you have a downhill putt, walk to the other side of the hole and look up the hill to your ball for the most accurate view of the slope's severity.

2   Next you need to know if you're faced with

side slope which will cause your ball to roll left or right of the hole. To read this correctly, pick out the low side of your putt and position yourself about halfway between your ball and the hole and look up the slope to make your judgment.

All putts break to the hole

Having completed your walk around the hole you'll have a good idea of the type of putt you are facing. If you are putting across a side slope, you'll need to aim your putt away from the hole if you want it to have a chance to go in. The idea is to make every putt a straight putt and let the slope carry the ball to, rather than away from, the hole. To do so, determine how much you think the slope will cause the ball to break—say, it's five inches. In this scenario, you'll pick a target five inches on the high side of the hole and putt your ball to this target. If you've calculated correctly, your ball will start five inches above the hole and gradually fall down the slope and into the hole.

When you determine the correct line to putt along, the slope of the green will take the ball to the hole.

Summary

The fascinating part of golf is that no two situations are the same, especially on the putting surface. As you gain putting experience, the judgments you make will be more accurate but the challenge never ends. Hopefully, your putting stroke will become automatic but, with its infinite variations, there will never be anything automatic about actually playing the game of golf. That's what makes golf so much fun for all of us.

Chapter six

Chipping

When you miss a shot to the green by just a couple of yards, you have entered the chipping zone—an area within five yards of the green, relative to your target line. The object of chipping is to clear a small obstacle, the rough and fringe around the green, with a low shot that lands about one yard on the green and rolls to the hole like a putt.

In essence, the chip shot is a putt with a lofted iron.

The advantages of chipping

In the chipping zone the amount of rough area you need to clear changes for every chip, but even from the maximum distance of five yards, you won't have much obstacle to carry. From this distance, it's advantageous to choose the low, running chip shot rather than the lofted pitch shot for the following reasons.

1   It is easier to control a rolling ball.

2   It is easier to land a ball on a target only a few yards from you than to fly the ball to a distant target well into the green.

3   The chip shot employs the more accurate stroke motion of putting rather than the more difficult swing motion used in pitching.

4   Since the ball rolls along the green like a putt you can study the break and play it.

These advantages make chipping almost as accurate as putting, and therefore each chip offers an opportunity to hole your shot or be right around the hole. Even a badly-struck chip gets you within the vicinity of the hole, whereas a badly-struck pitch from the same distance could put you in the bunker on the other side of the green.

Pitch, chip or putt—how you decide

Putting the ball should always be your first choice because, since the ball never gets airborne, you have the least margin for error. From just off the green, putt the ball if the grass between your ball and the green is short and the contour of the ground is flat.

If putting is not an option, your next choice is to chip the ball, but be sure you are actually within the five-yard chipping zone. You may find your ball sits just a few yards off the nearest part of the green, but when you look along your actual target line there's much more than five yards between your ball and the edge of the green. In this case, you need to hit a short pitch which produces the loft necessary to clear this more significant obstacle.

You will hit a chip shot when five yards or less lies between your ball and the edge of the green along your target line. To chip the ball with maximum efficiency, you'll use your putting motion and a variety of irons to adjust the distance your ball travels.

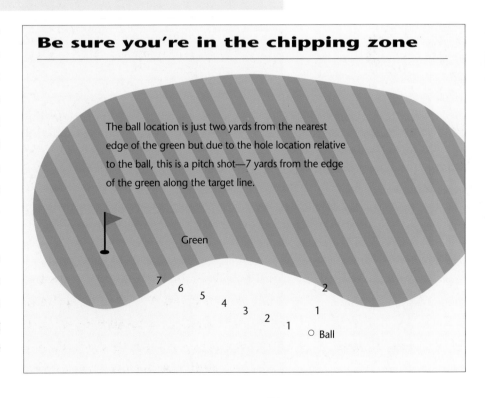

Be sure you're in the chipping zone

The ball location is just two yards from the nearest edge of the green but due to the hole location relative to the ball, this is a pitch shot—7 yards from the edge of the green along the target line.

Green

The flight-to-roll ratio

In our method, along with the best chippers of the ball in professional golf, we advocate making use of every iron in your bag, depending on the chipping situation that you face. As you have seen, every chip you hit flies in the air a short distance, lands about one yard on the green, then rolls to the hole like a putt. Therefore each chip has a different ratio of flight time versus roll time.

■ For example, when your ball lies three yards from your landing area and your landing area is, say, six yards from the hole, then the ball's flight-to-roll ratio is one part flight and two parts roll (a ratio of 3:6 reduces to 1:2).

■ In another scenario, you may have two yards to your landing area with 14 yards from your landing area to the hole, a ratio of one part flight to seven parts roll (2:14 reduces to 1:7).

The fact that each of your irons has a different amount of loft means that you can choose the iron best suited to the flight-to-roll ratio you face. Rather than trying to force one club to fit every situation, you can use the iron with the specific loft to produce the desired flight-to-roll ratio. A three iron chip flies low and rolls a long distance—the perfect flight-to-roll ratio for a situation where you have very little distance to the green but a long distance to the hole. At the other end of the spectrum, a sand wedge chip flies high and doesn't roll as far—a perfect ratio for an equal amount of obstacle and roll.

1 When you choose the correct iron for each chipping situation, you can land the ball about a yard · onto the green and let it roll to the hole like a putt.

2 The benefit of a properly executed chip shot is that you can read the green as you would in putting, and figure the break into your chipping strategy.

Club selection chart

The club selection chart relates the ratio between the amounts of flight versus roll you get when chipping with each club.

Club	Flight	Roll
Sand wedge (11-iron)	1 part	1 part
Pitching wedge (10-iron)	1 part	2 parts
9-iron	1 part	3 parts
8-iron	1 part	4 parts
7-iron	1 part	5 parts
6-iron	1 part	6 parts
5-iron	1 part	7 parts
4-iron	1 part	8 parts
3-iron	1 part	9 parts

Since every chip shot requires some flight time to land on the green, one and two irons are not considered because they don't have enough loft. If you don't carry a three or four iron you can use the next club down and stroke it more firmly.

Figuring your flight-to-roll ratio

To figure your flight-to-roll ratio, take two measurements and plug them into a simple formula.

The two constants

Keep in mind that there are two constants for every chip. They are as follows:

- The landing area one yard on the green.
- The number 12.

As you have learned, this landing area is easy to hit because it's only a few yards away, and in case you mis-hit the ball, one yard allows enough margin for error to still have your ball land safely on the green.

Study the chart to understand the second constant—the number 12. Twelve is the sum of the club number and the roll added together.

The two variables

In addition to the two constants, there are two variables, which are as follows:

- The distance the ball flies in the air.
- The distance the ball rolls to the hole.

To determine the club for the shot, calculate the ratio (or proportion) of flight to roll as below.

The procedure

1   Once you've determined your target line, pace off the number of steps from your ball to your landing area, which is one yard on the green. This determines your first variable: the amount the ball flies.

2   Keeping your stride width consistent, next pace off the distance from your landing area to the hole to determine your second variable: the amount the ball rolls. You now have enough information to calculate the flight-to-roll ratio using some simple arithmetic.

3   Create a fraction with your flight time on the top and your roll time on the bottom. Then reduce the fraction to 1 over the appropriate number.

The flight-to-roll ratio *continued*

Once you reduce your flight-to-roll ratio, you are always left with one part flight to so many parts roll, giving you the proportion between the two.

Although every chip shot has a different recipe, if you understand the basis of the ratio in this way you can take a short cut to figure the ratio for your chips. Go to a practice green and place your ball at different distances from various holes within the chipping zone. Take a good look at the distance your ball needs to fly to your landing area and mark it in your mind as one part. Then ask yourself: how many of those parts fit in the distance from the landing area to the hole. You will automatically have your ratio, say, one part flight with four parts roll. Subtract four from the constant 12 and you've got an eight iron. Then pace off the distances and see how well your eyes worked. Do this with all the balls you've laid out and then see how often you come up with the right ratio just by eyeing it. It won't take long before you can get it right every time.

For example, the ratio of 5 steps of flight time over 15 steps of roll time, reduces to 1 over 3, one part flight and three parts roll.

4   The next step is to subtract the denominator (3) from the constant (12) to identify your chipping club, which in our example is a nine iron. **Note:** if the ratio isn't evenly reducible, adjust the denominator to the nearest number that gives you a ratio that's easy to calculate in your head. Thus 3 over 13 would be adjusted to 3 over 12. You should also adjust the club depending on the slope of the green.

Chipping uphill—add roll by choosing a five rather than a six iron.

If it's downhill, subtract roll by going from a six to a seven iron.

Exact measurements

The object of walking off the distance of your flight and roll is not to come up with exact measurements. You are simply trying to find the ratio between the amount your ball needs to fly and the amount it needs to roll. Rarely will a situation present itself where, for example, your ball is precisely three yards from your landing area and then exactly nine yards to the hole. The general proportion between the two is what's important, and should guide you as you use logic to adjust the numbers.

Once you can see the ratio between flight and roll, then you will choose the right club for each situation on the golf course.

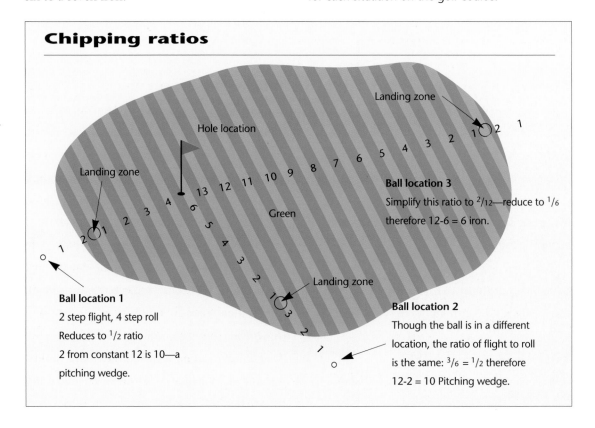

Chipping ratios

Ball location 1
2 step flight, 4 step roll
Reduces to $^1/_2$ ratio
2 from constant 12 is 10—a
pitching wedge.

Ball location 2
Though the ball is in a different location, the ratio of flight to roll is the same: $^3/_6 = ^1/_2$ therefore 12-2 = 10 Pitching wedge.

Ball location 3
Simplify this ratio to $^2/_{12}$—reduce to $^1/_6$ therefore 12-6 = 6 iron.

Hole location
Landing zone
Green
Landing zone
Landing zone

The set up

When done correctly, the putting stroke is the most accurate motion in golf and therefore it is a good idea to think of your chip as a putt. Once you know what club you need for a chip shot, you will adapt it in three ways so that you can use your putting motion.

■ Raise your iron on its toe so that it is upright like your putter. This moves you closer to the ball with your eyes over the target line as in putting. When you raise any club on its toe, the face aims to the right so you'll need to turn the toe in toward the ball until the top line of your club face is perpendicular to your target line. You don't use the top line as a guide in non-chipping situations (use the leading edge to aim the club face for full shots) but it is quite useful for chipping.

■ Grip down on your iron to make it the same length as your putter and use your putting grip. Since you'll use irons of various lengths, this means you'll grip down a lot on the long-shafted

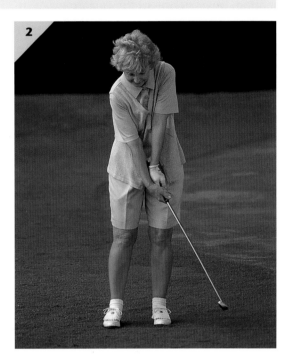

four iron and not much at all on the pitching wedge. The idea is to make the various iron lengths consistent with the length of your putter. With your putting grip, you'll minimize the possibility of wrist action—the great destroyer of the putting/chipping motion. If you use your wrists, essentially you change clubs during your swing since wrist action decreases loft in the backswing and increases the loft on the downswing. This negates the benefit of selecting the iron with the precise loft for your flight-to-roll situation.

■ You will use the iron just like you do your putter, a pendulum motion which is controlled by your upper body, with no lower body and no wrist action.

1 Make your chipping iron like your putter by raising it on its toe.

2 Eliminate the wrist flip error from your chipping motion, otherwise you'll add loft to the club during your swing.

Note

Although a chip has minimal flight time, you'll need a set up which creates the descending motion necessary for some loft. The chipping set up encourages a descending motion and allows you to simply execute your putting stroke.

The set up *continued*

For a chip shot, your set up will change but the motion you employ will be identical to your putting stroke.

Stance width

Since the stroke motion requires no lower body motion, your stance width is narrow. As in putting, lower body movement is unnecessary and detrimental to your putting stroke. You don't have time for a weight transfer and you certainly don't need the power it provides.

Open stance

In chipping, you want to hit the ball with a descending blow so place 80 percent of your weight on your left foot. Drop your left foot back from the target line into an open position and allow your weight to settle naturally into your left hip. This distribution anchors your lower body and encourages your weight to start, stay and finish on your left side throughout your stroke.

Ball position

Position the ball opposite the inside of your right foot, with your hands set ahead by your left thigh. With your weight on your left side, you easily produce the proper angle of attack, a naturally descending motion, without trying to "hit down" on the ball. Since the ball is well back in your stance, your shoulders close as a result, so draw your left foot back from the target line until your shoulders arrive at the necessary square address position.

Distance from the ball

Although the distance you stand from the ball depends on your body build, you should stand close enough so that your eyes are over the target line and your arms hang freely, straight down from your shoulders. If done correctly, the ball is close to your feet, generally about six inches away.

Plan your chip like a putt

Read the green and visualize your chip shot just as you would a putt. You should see in your mind's eye the target line, where you want the ball to begin its roll and also the spot where you want the ball to finish. With the proper club selection and the appropriate adjustments all you need to think about is how hard you would hit a putt of the same distance. This may sound obvious but if you're faced with a curving chip, plan it like you would a putt. Set up on the line you want the ball to start on and stroke the chip down this line, allowing the slope of the green to take the ball to the hole.

The stroke

Once you've set up correctly, your backswing is all shoulders and arms, without any conscious wrist action. Your shoulders control the stroke in both directions just as they do in the putting stroke. Throughout the chipping motion, your lower body stays quiet but not rigid. Actually, on longer chip shots you will need some turn so your arms can swing freely without bumping into your sides, but what movement there is should be reactive.

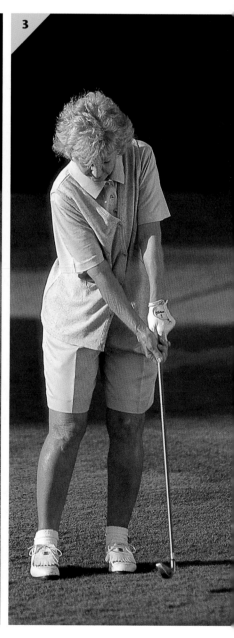

Chapter seven

Pitching

A pitch shot is nothing more than a miniature version of your full swing, used when you are close enough to the green where a full swing, even with your most lofted club, would produce too much distance. In the pitching zone, you will need a lofted shot that lands softly after it clears the obstacles that surround most greens.

Since loft is your main objective, choose your sand wedge for your pitch shots. In addition to loft, your sand wedge is useful because of its weight and its bounce. Since it is your heaviest club, your sand wedge helps cut through deep or

With help from her superb pitching skills, Tour star Helen Alfredsson fired a record-breaking 63 in the 1994 US Women's Open Championship.

wiry rough found around most greens. And bounce, the rudder-like protrusion on the sole, keeps your club sliding smoothly through the grass. Your pitching wedge does not have this feature so if you use it, you run the risk of snagging the sharp leading edge against the ground. In addition, you will not gain the benefit of the increased loft and weight of your sand wedge.

The four absolutes

Like every other shot in golf, how you set up to the ball dictates the quality of your shots. To consistently pitch the ball well, follow the four absolutes for every pitch shot as outlined below.

Aiming the club face

At address, make sure your club face aims at your target because the ball deflects in the direction in which the club face aims. This sounds obvious but, as you will learn, most pitch shots require that you open your stance so you will need to be careful that this adjustment does not disturb the aim of your club. Simply follow your pre-shot routine where you take care of your aim first and then arrange your body; so it's aim, then align.

Positioning of hands

The butt of the club must point at the center line of your body in order to maintain proper loft on the club face. Many golfers set their hands well ahead of the ball at address which effectively decreases the loft of the club and, consequently, the height of their shots. In addition, hands ahead brings the leading edge of the club into play, negating the positive effect of bounce. Even worse, it sets the hosel dangerously close to the ball, encouraging the dreaded shank, a shot that goes severely to the right due to contact with the hosel of the club rather than the club face.

An even-length swing

The distance you swing the club back and through is equal in length; if you use a three-quarter backswing, match it with a three-quarter follow through. When the situation calls for a half backswing, it also calls for a follow through that is half of your normal one. Obviously when you contact the ball your club loses speed because it has just run into an obstacle (the ball) so in order to satisfy the same length-swing concept, your brain learns by trial and error how much to accelerate the club to give you the same-length

1 Though your body turns in response to the motion of the swing, the pressure of your weight should stay over your left leg for short pitch shots.

2 The momentum of the downswing provides natural acceleration to the pitch shot.

3 The proper set up fundamentals and an even tempo result in a swing of equal distance back and through.

The four absolutes *continued*

swing on both sides of the ball. Once you have the concept, you learn the execution by practice.

Controlling your tempo is the key to accomplishing an even-length swing. Although the natural forces of the swing motion cause the club to accelerate as it nears impact, you must keep your tempo even to achieve uniform length back and through. When your backswing is long and your follow through short, you have actually decelerated the club and you will tend to hit the ground behind the ball. With a short backswing and a long follow through there is a tendency to hit the middle of the ball producing a long, low-running shot, just the opposite of the high, soft shot you planned for. So maintaining an even-length swing is contingent upon your ability to maintain your tempo and, when you do, you will contact the ball cleanly with no unpleasant surprises.

Down the shoulder line

The club always swings down your shoulder line. Remember that we said that the pitch was a miniature swing, and in the full swing, the club must be allowed to swing down the shoulder line. You can test this by assuming your golf posture without a club, letting your arms hang straight down guided only by the pull of gravity. Now swing your shoulders as you would in a real golf swing and you will find that your arms and hands naturally follow the direction of your shoulders. If you try to over-control the club, you may push it outside or pull it inside the line of your shoulders. When this happens, you will have difficulty squaring the club face at impact because you have drastically changed the club-to-body relationship you established at address.

Distance control

The first objective is to determine the distance you want your ball to travel. If you have less than five yards to clear before you can get on the green, you will want to chip the ball (see page 80). From outside this area, categorize your pitch shots as short, medium or long, based on the distance you hit your sand wedge with a full swing. There is no rule on how far the pitch should fly because it depends on the strength and accomplishment of the player; whereas for one golfer a medium pitch might be 50 feet, for another it might be 50 yards—the point is that it depends on you. You will progressively change the distance the ball travels simply by adjusting your set up.

Set up adjustments

Combine the following three set-up adjustments to adjust the distance of your pitches:

1   You can shorten the length of your lever, i.e. the club shaft.

2   You can restrict the turn of your body by narrowing your stance.

Your next step is to control the trajectory of your pitch shots. One solution is to add a lob wedge to your clubs since it's additional loft produce higher flying shots that stop quickly.

Change the trajectory of your shots by adjusting your ball position with your wedges. Keeping the "four absolutes" in mind, you can hit higher, softer shots by moving the ball forward in your stance. This ball position opens your shoulders and aims the club face left of the target. Adjust the face so it aims back at the target, and let your arms swing down your open shoulder line. This creates a slicing motion that imparts additional backspin on the ball to make your shots fly higher and land softer.

To hit pitch shots that fly lower and roll more, do the opposite. Move the ball back in your stance. This closes your shoulders and aims your club face right of your target. Adjust your club face so it points back to the target, and swing along your closed shoulder line. Doing so puts less backspin on the ball and produces lower, more running pitch shots.

3 You can reduce the length of your backswing by opening your stance.

Although you will have to practice to get a feel for your specific distances, the following example illustrates the method.

Long pitch shots

Say, you hit your sand wedge 60 yards with your full swing. When you have a 30-yard shot you will reduce the distance the ball travels in the following manner.

■ Shorten the length of your club by gripping down about one inch. The shorter the lever, then the shorter your swing arc and the less club

head speed and distance you will generate.

■ Narrow your stance slightly and then drop your left foot back so that your left toe is even with the ball of your right foot. From this position, the length of your backswing shortens because your open foot position literally blocks your body from making its full turn. In addition, if you pay attention to your balance, you will realize that to swing in balance you must reduce the length of your swing because you have narrowed the platform (your feet) from which you are swinging. By limiting your motion, these set up adjustments reduce the distance of your shot—from 60 to 30 yards in this scenario.

Since the term pitch shot implies something less than a full swing, slightly modify your full swing set up for those long, but not quite full, pitches. To do so, narrow and open your stance a bit and grip down slightly on the club. From this set up, your swing is naturally shorter as is the distance the ball flies.

Distance control *continued*

Short pitch shots

For your shortest pitch shots, you'll make significant set up adjustments. Take a very narrow open stance and put your hands on the club so your right hand is almost touching the shaft. From this position, your swing will be naturally shorter.

As you need to shorten your distance even more, you will progressively shorten the shaft, narrow your stance and open your stance. For a medium-length pitch, grip down to the middle of the grip, progressively narrow your stance, and open your stance by dropping your left foot back until your toes are even with the arch of your right foot.

For your shortest distance pitches, your hands are as low as possible on the grip, with your feet only a few inches apart and your left toe even with your right heel. Since the club is so short, you will also need to increase your knee flex to make sure you get down to the ball.

Pitching guidelines

Obviously a certain amount of practice and feel is necessary to learn the variety of distances you will face in the pitching zone, but these guidelines give you a strong foundation for short-, medium- and long-range distances. In pitching, what separates a Tour player from the average player is the ability to hit the ball within a yard or two of their actual yardage. So if your handicap is high, you will take a giant step toward lowering it if you learn to hit short-, medium- and long-distance pitches on command. If you're a low handicapper, you probably already have good touch around the greens and these guidelines can help you to

hone your distance skills and to eliminate any inconsistencies in your pitching.

An underhand throwing motion

The three distance control adjustments you make to your set up, and the resultant swing, are similar to the natural adjustments you make when you toss a ball different distances. For a short-distance toss, you face your target with a narrow stance and your motion is upper-body oriented, mostly an arm swing. For a short-distance pitch, you've learned that your stance is narrow and open and the length of your swing matches the amount your set up position can support. As you need to throw the ball farther and farther, you'll naturally widen and square off your stance to allow a fuller body motion—the same adjustment you make for pitching.

Power tip

If you are trying to add distance and power to your full game, take careful note of the adjustments made to reduce the distance of a pitch shot, and be sure that they're not a part of your full swing set up! An open stance with your driver is just as effective in reducing distance as it is in pitching.

Remember that from a short pitch set up you will only be able to make a short swing. If you find you're losing your balance, you can be sure you're trying to swing the club longer than necessary.

93

Pitching technique

Once you know how to take distance off your pitches by adjusting your set up, your main concern is to let this set up dictate the length of your swing. All the other features of your set up—grip, posture, ball position, aim and alignment—are the same as with your full swing.

Low hands, high club head

If you swing in balance, you will find that for a short pitch, your hands never rise above waist high; for a medium-length pitch they rise to the middle of your chest; and for the long pitch they swing to about shoulder high. But remember to swing your arms as you would at the start of your full swing, although you never actually lift your

Good pitchers of the ball keep their hands low and elevate the club head with their wrists. If you hit your pitch shots fat and thin, there's a good chance that you're lifting your arms and hands instead of just letting them swing.

arms to these positions. Therefore as your hands and arms stay low, your club head is elevated above your shoulders by the setting (cocking) of your wrists. This gives you the club head height you need for sufficient backswing length but keeps your arms and hands under control. This relationship of low hands and high club head is the hallmark of a good pitcher.

Weight shift and rotation

For pitch shots that require a stance narrower than hip width, your weight stays in your left hip joint, where it settles naturally when you drop your left foot back. As you swing, keep your weight left; there's no time in a short swing for a weight transfer and you don't want the power it would provide. But this doesn't mean that you should stand perfectly still and just swing your arms up and down. Let your body rotate around your left hip axis as you swing the club.

■ For long pitches, you'll have a good deal of rotation during the backswing.

■ For medium distances, you will have some rotation.

■ For short pitches, you will have very little rotation.

The short shot is primarily an arm swing to waist high but when the shot is longer your shoulders are included. As the shot continues to increase in length, the final power source, the hips, become the focal point of your swing and a weight shift from hip to hip takes place as your hands swing to shoulder height.

The swing

The triangle formed by your shoulders and arms remains intact until waist high with the butt of your club pointing at your navel. There is no wrist cock until the weight of your swinging club head creates a natural hinging of your wrists. Only when your right elbow begins to fold do your wrists hinge; and the more folding and hinging, the higher the ball flies.

Your lower body initiates the return of your club head to the ball by rotating your left hip and right knee back through the address position. This keeps you hitting down and through the ball. Never allow the club head to pass your hands through impact. The most common mistake that is made in pitching is to abruptly stop the arms at impact in an attempt to put a "hit" on the ball. When this happens, your left wrist collapses, sending the club head past your hands in a flipping action that makes solid contact impossible. You can avoid being a "flipper" by keeping your arms moving well into your follow through. To do this effectively you must keep your left hip rotating and your right knee moving as you swing through the ball.

Allow your coil to dictate the amount of swing produced, with your hands finishing at the same height as they were at the top of your swing. This way, the length of your swing always matches the length of the shot: short swing for a short shot, long swing for a long shot. Thus your backswing and through swing are a mirror image of each other.

Good pitchers of the ball have minimal leg action during the backswing while their upper body creates the length and leverage necessary for the shot. During the forward swing, however, there's a good deal of leg action with the right knee moving very aggressively to the target. This "quiet-then-active" sequence is often reversed by the poor pitcher of the ball so that the lower body (hips and legs) is very active on the backswing but dead during the forward swing, leaving the hands and arms to over-manipulate the club.

Chapter eight

Bunkers

In a greenside bunker, you will use your sand wedge but how you use it will differ depending on your lie. When your ball sits on top of the sand, you will use the splash shot technique, and when it is buried in the sand you will use the blast shot technique. Both these techniques are explained in this chapter.

Though many amateurs fear bunker shots, proper technique can make them one of the easiest shots in golf. The keys are to swing with a slicing action and hit the sand before you hit the ball. By setting up correctly, these keys will become automatic to you and you'll face your bunker shots with confidence.

Splash shots

You can visualize the splash shot technique if you picture your ball sitting on the center of a dollar bill resting on the sand. The idea is to slice a thin layer of sand, about the size of the bill, out from under the ball. Your club never contacts the ball; rather the ball rides out of the bunker on a cushion, or splash, of sand. Your sand wedge has bounce, a specially designed bulge in its sole which allows your club to skim through the sand in this manner.

The technique

■ To maximize the bounce, always open your club face so it points right of your target. Opening the face also increases the loft, so the shorter the shot the more you'll open the club face.

■ Be careful to open the club face before you take your golf grip. To do so, aim the club face to the right of the target (an open position), then take your grip without changing the position of the club face. If you take your grip first and then roll your arms to open the club face, you won't be able to keep the face open at impact because your arms will return to their natural position as you swing. Hence the club face returns to the ball in a square or, worse, a closed position—just what you don't want when you need to slide your club under the ball.

■ Next, while keeping the butt end of your club pointing at the center line of your body, open

your stance by drawing your left foot away from your target line in an amount sufficient to re-aim your club face back at the target. By opening your stance, you encourage your weight to settle on your left side and you'll keep it there throughout your swing, just as you do with all your short greenside shots. This stabilizes your lower body and insures a descending motion and full finish.

A common error

Before you swing, be careful not to tilt your head and spine toward your right shoulder, a common mistake made by those who think it's necessary to lift the ball or help it up. The weight of your head is enough to cause your head and spine to lean toward your right shoulder, and so does the rest of your body weight, tilting your entire body out of position. Position your head correctly and trust that the ball will ride out on a wave of sand. A descending motion rather than a lifting motion is the only way to hit consistently good splash shots.

1 For the splash shot, imagine cutting a slice of sand that's about the size of a dollar bill out of the bunker.

2 Though the club face aims at the target, you'll set your body in an open position for the splash shot.

Splash shots *continued*

■ Since you want to contact the sand behind the ball, rather than the ball itself, position the ball forward in your stance off your left heel. This opens your shoulders and, since your club swings along your shoulder line, you are set for an outside-to-in swing path that slices the ball out of the sand.

■ Dig your feet into the sand for stability. Digging in lowers your feet in relationship to the level of the ball, guaranteeing that you'll hit the sand first, a necessary feature of the splash

shot. But be careful to stand slightly farther from the ball because when you dig your feet in, you effectively move the hosel of the club closer to the ball.

■ With your weight on your left side throughout your swing most of your motion occurs in your upper body, but don't misinterpret this to mean that you just lift your arms. Let your arms and shoulders swing the club back along your shoulder line and continue this rotation to a full finish.

Though the distance to the hole is relatively short, the splash shot calls for a rather full swing which is necessary to propel the ball out of the bunker on a cushion of sand.

Summary

Even when golfers make a good set up, the most common error is to pick the club up with their arms while their body stays frozen in place From this position, the club head returns on a steep path and digs deeply into the sand, making it impossible to splash through the sand and end in a full finish. Keep in mind the concept of splashing the ball on to the green by slicing a thin layer of sand out from under the ball. Though a certain amount of trust is required to take a full swing for such a short shot, once you see your results your confidence increases rapidly.

Buried bunker shots

When your ball is buried deep in the sand, either in a fairway or greenside bunker, you'll need to blast or explode the ball from this lie. Although it looks difficult, the procedure for extracting it is quite simple. Once you know the blast shot technique, the only difficulty is accepting that you can't advance the ball very far from a fairway bunker, and you can't control your distance well from a greenside bunker.

To play this shot successfully you'll make a deeper cut into the sand than you would for a splash shot but, once again, the ball rides out on a layer of sand. To execute the buried lie shot, you'll need a descending motion, so although it's tempting, be sure to clear your mind of any thoughts about lifting the ball from this lie.

■ For the blast shot, position the ball back in your stance toward your right foot. With the ball in this position you'll need to close your club face. As a consequence, you'll expose the leading edge and eliminate the bounce, the ideal club specifications for digging your club into the sand.

■ Drop your left foot back from the target line to anchor your weight on your left side. From this position, swing the club up with your arms and hit down behind the ball aggressively. With a

Reading *your lie*

Sometimes it's difficult to decide whether you need the splash shot or buried lie technique. If the front of the ball (toward the target) is buried a bit, but the back of it doesn't have a lot of sand behind it, you can still use the splash shot technique. If the back of the ball is below the surface of the sand, always use the buried lie technique.

Unlike the splash shot, you'll play the ball well back in your stance when it is buried in the bunker.

Buried bunker shots *continued*

closed club face and a descending blow, your club digs into the sand causing the ball to pop out.

■ Since your club digs into the sand, don't try to follow through. Done correctly, you'll leave your club head low with a very limited follow through. Too often golfers try to lift the ball out of a buried lie, an impossible task that results in a more deeply buried ball. Since a good bit of force is necessary to remove the ball, expect it to roll once on the green. Your goal from this awful lie is simply to get out of the bunker. With the proper technique, you'll do so with ease.

Fairway bunker shots

Middle- to high-handicap golfers often dread the fairway bunker shot. Although the shot itself isn't difficult, most problems occur when the conditions of the shot aren't properly evaluated.

Evaluate the "three L's"

Before making your club selection, first assess the conditions of play by checking the "three L's:"

- The **lie** of your golf ball.
- The **lip** of the bunker.
- The **length** of the shot.

The lie of the ball determines the type of shot you can play. The lip, the elevated edge of the bunker, requires that you choose a club with ample loft for clearance. If the first two conditions are favorable, only then can you consider the total length of the shot.

If your ball is buried in the sand, you'll have to hit a blast shot with your sand wedge, regardless of your total distance. If your ball is sitting nicely on top of the sand, next check the height of the bunker's lip. Be certain you choose a club with enough loft to safely clear the edge of the bunker (see side bar). Once you have evaluated the lie and the lip, only then can you consider the total length you want your ball to travel. The fairway bunker technique shortens the distance you normally hit your irons, so be sure to include that in your calculations. If your total distance normally requires an eight iron, you'll need to hit a seven iron from a fairway bunker. But if you find the height of the lip of the bunker requires an eight iron for clearance, then that is the club you will have to use for this shot.

The technique

The worst mistake you can make in a fairway bunker is not to get the ball out. Evaluating the "three L's" is the first step in preventing this error. Next, unless you're an expert, never use more than a four iron in a fairway bunker. Long irons

Visualizing *the loft*

To visualize the trajectory of an iron try the following technique. Choose the iron that you think will clear the lip of the bunker. Lay it down in the grass, adjacent to your position in the sand, with the butt end of the club pointing in the direction you want your ball to fly. Step on the club face until the back of the club is against the ground and the butt end rises up. The angle of the shaft indicates the approximate amount of loft that iron produces. Remember, your club can't touch the sand according to the rules, so don't try this in the bunker unless you're just practicing.

For fairway bunker shots, play the ball toward the middle of your stance and keep your weight more on your left side while you swing.

Fairway bunker shots *continued*

and fairway woods are difficult to get airborne and there's a tendency to help them up, especially from the sand. This usually results in a fat shot, where the club contacts the sand first and the ball advances only a few feet.

For this reason, regardless of the club you choose, your priority in a fairway bunker is to prevent the fat shot. Although you'll take almost a normal swing, your set up is dedicated to making sure you hit the ball cleanly or even a bit thin—anything but fat.

■ Begin by gripping down on your club about an inch.

■ Position the ball in the middle of your stance and stand slightly farther from the ball than normal, just enough so that you are addressing the ball more toward the toe of the club. From this position, you'll avoid hitting the sand behind the ball, the most costly, and fear-inspiring, error in a fairway bunker.

■ Since sand is an unstable platform for a full shot, widen and open your stance so your weight settles more on your left side, thus encouraging a relatively quiet lower body during the shot.

■ Dig your left foot in the sand slightly and wedge your right foot into the sand with your right knee angled in toward the target. This position encourages a descending motion, enabling you to pick the ball cleanly. Although your stance is open, be sure your shoulders are square.

The swing

You are now set up to avoid the fat shot. If you've chosen a club with ample loft you can even hit the ball a little thin and still be successful.

■ You'll modify your swing simply by making a three-quarter motion so most of your weight remains on your left side throughout. By reducing weight transfer, you decrease the risk that you'll

Adjusting for uneven lies in greenside bunkers

Downhill lies

1 For the downhill lie, play the ball slightly forward of the center in your stance (practice will tell you exactly how much) rather than off your left instep as you would for a normal greenside sand shot.

2 Since the ball is below your feet, the lowest point of your swing is back of the center of your stance and that's exactly where you want your club head to enter the sand—behind the ball, insuring that you hit the sand first.

3 Next draw your right foot back so your stance is slightly closed to the target. This levels your hips and makes your lower body posture as normal as possible under the conditions. Check to make sure at least 75 percent of your weight is on your left side, where it should remain throughout your swing.

4 Lastly, tilt your shoulders so they match the angle of the slope. Then make

sure to swing down the slope as if your club head was going to land at the bottom of the bunker.

5 Under no circumstances should you try to lift the ball with your swing. Just stay with the shot and allow the ball to come out on a cushion of sand. And don't get greedy; give yourself some room because this shot runs once it hits the green. Instead, visualize the run, plan for it and then let it ramble.

Ball above feet

When the ball is above your feet, do exactly the opposite, i.e. move the ball back and open your stance. Adjust your shoulders to the hill and then swing up the slope. The ball comes out very high and soft so you'll have to carry it all the way to the hole.

sink into the sand at the top of your swing or sway off the ball—a sure way to hit sand before you contact the ball.

■ The key here is to keep your spine angle while you swing. Too many golfers try to lift the ball out of the sand by dropping their back shoulder down toward the ground, a sure way to catch the sand first and leave your shot well short of your target.

Though your body responds to the motion of your swing, your weight stays mostly on your left side with your left leg serving as your axis for rotation.

Chapter nine

Uneven lies

When your ball is perched on the side of a hill so that your feet and the ball are not on the same level, you have what is known as an uneven lie. At first glance, these lies appear difficult but if you know how to adjust your set up you'll be able to make a fairly normal golf swing that results in an accurate shot. There are several adjustments which are specific to each of these situations but rather than trying to memorize them, you should understand how they affect your balance, your golf swing and

Simple set up adjustments minimize the effects of uneven lies.

your ball flight. This way you'll remember the necessary adjustments more easily.

There are four basic types of uneven lies:

1 Ball above your feet.

2 Ball below your feet.

3 Downhill lies.

4 Uphill lies.

Gravity pulls your body down the hill, thereby

challenging your ability to make a balanced swing. Although we'll show you how to adjust your set up to compensate, you'll still need to make a three-quarter swing motion from these uneven lies.

The effects of uneven lies

1   The ball follows the direction of the slope.

2   The club face points in the direction of the slope.

3   You'll lose your balance down the slope.

4   The bottom of your swing arc is altered by the slope.

5   The path and plane of your swing are altered by the slope.

Although uneven lies tend to be opposites of each other there are general adjustments standard for all. Your first priority is to protect your balance by anchoring yourself into the hill. Then angle your shoulders to match the slope so that you can swing with the contour of the hill. Each lie causes your club to bottom-out sooner or later than normal so you need to adjust your ball position accordingly. And, finally, by opening or closing your stance, you neutralize the effect of the slope by returning your hips to a level, balanced position. Once you've made the correct adjustments in your set up, the only adjustment you'll make to your swing is limiting it to a smooth, three-quarter motion.

Choice
of club

Unless it is a very subtle slope, an uneven lie is no place for a long iron or fairway wood. The distance may require your three wood but your course management skills should tell you to play a safety shot back to level land and let your short game save your par. It would be a very unusual instance for the average player to use more than a five iron from a severe slope.

Ball above your feet

When the ball is above your feet, you're forced to swing more around your body, on a flatter plane, causing your shots to fly left of target, usually with a right-to-left spin. To offset this, you should make the following modifications. Since all good swings depend on balance the first order of business is to neutralize the tendency to be pulled backward.

1   Flex your knees into the hill with your weight toward the balls of your feet and leave it there to anchor your swing. Also be sure to keep your weight on the inside of your right foot. The danger is that, as your swing progresses, the momentum of your turn will topple you backward down the hill, an error you can prevent if you're well anchored on your right side.

2   Take one more club and choke down since the slope moves the ball closer to you.

3   For the same reason, your club will contact the ground sooner so move the ball back in your stance. This way the ball will be there when your club head arrives.

4   To neutralize the tendency for your ball to go left, allow your shoulders to close, an alignment that aims your club face right of the target. With both your shoulders and your club face aimed right, your swing takes an in-to-out path that offsets the tendency for the ball to start left.

5   Once you are aimed properly, simply swing the club, allowing your set up to determine your swing path.

Ball above your feet *continued*

Summary

Stand more upright with your knees flexed into the hill. Because you are closer to the ball, slide your hands down on the grip about one-and-a-half inches. Once you have planned your shot, sole the club behind the ball to establish your posture and the plane of your swing, with your ball two inches back in the middle of your stance. Now make a three-quarter swing, concentrating on keeping your balance from start to finish.

When the ball is above your feet, swing the club more around your body to produce the flatter swing plane your club shaft dictates at address. Also, shorten the length of your swing in order to stay in balance through the shot.

Ball below your feet

When the ball is lower than your feet, your swing is more up and down than it is around. With a more upright swing, your club face tends to point to the right of the target at impact curving your shot from left to right. Without adjustment, when the ball is below your feet, you can expect a shot that flies low and to the right.

When the ball is below your feet, swing the club more up and down, rather than around your body, to match the swing plane your upright club shaft establishes at address. Stand close enough to the ball so your weight can settle toward your heels and into the hillside. This helps you to maintain your balance on this difficult lie.

Ball below your feet *continued*

■ Prior to arranging your feet, sole your club flush with the slope, allowing the shaft to be more upright than normal. The lie of your club establishes the plane of your swing and the posture you'll need at address. The upright position puts the club on its toe, effectively aiming the club face to the right.

■ Since the ball is farther from you, the bottom of your arc occurs later in your swing and to catch the ball solidly and give your club face time to square up to the target, you must move the ball forward in your stance. This aligns your shoulders left of the target, offsetting the tendency for the ball to start to the right of your target.

■ When the ball is below your feet, it's actually farther from you, so stand closer to it with a wider stance and more knee flex, lowering yourself to the ball. Pinch your knees inward and turn your feet in (pigeon toed) to minimize side-to-side motion.

■ Settle your weight onto your heels and into the hillside to further anchor your lower body. Remember that since the hill tries to pull you forward onto your toes as you swing, you should make every effort to stay on your heels from start to finish.

Summary

Assume a wider stance and sole the club to establish both your plane and posture. Stand more over the ball and pigeon toe your feet as you flex your knees into the hill. Position your ball forward in your stance from where you would normally position it for a level lie (about two inches). Your swing is a three-quarter motion, concentrating on keeping your balance throughout the swing

Uphill and downhill lies

When adjusting your body to an uphill or downhill slope, visualize balancing a table on the slope. In order to keep the table from tipping, you would level it by shortening the uphill legs. When your ball is on slopes in golf, you use the same principle by moving your uphill leg back, away from the target line to create a level hip turn. For downhill slopes, draw your right foot back away from the target line and increase the amount of flex in your right leg. Do the opposite for an uphill slope. And, since your shoulders dictate the path of your swing, angle them to match the slope of the hill, so your swing can follow the contour of the incline.

The amount you open or close your stance depends on the severity of the slope. For both uphill and downhill slopes, adjust your stance until your hips are level. For both types of lies the ball is played in the middle of your stance.

Uphill lies

On an uphill lie your ball is higher than your right foot and lower than your left. The slope acts as a launching pad, adding height to your shot along with a tendency for your ball to go to the left. When you sole your club, its effective loft is increased because of the slope. For these reasons, it is best to take more club from an uphill lie.

■ On an up slope, your left foot is drawn back from the target line, effectively shortening your left leg and leveling your hips. With your left foot dropped back, your weight settles comfortably into the hillside as an anchor for balance. Flare your left foot out to make it easier to turn through the shot. Since you want to swing up the slope (not into it), tilt your shoulders to mimic

On an uphill lie, drop your left foot back to level your hips. When you do, you will find that your weight settles into the hill for balance and you'll be able to turn through the shot more easily.

Uphill and downhill lies *continued*

"The righting instinct"

For good reason, no one likes to lose their balance and fall down. Fortunately, one of the strongest instincts in the human body is the righting instinct but it can be a detriment to your golf shots if it's triggered during your swing. When you bend your upper body to address a golf ball, it's important to create a counter balance with your lower body (see Chapter 2 on the Set Up). If you start your swing from an unbalanced position, the righting instinct forces you back in balance at some point during your swing. When you lose your balance, you change your relationship to the ball at the bottom of your swing arc, which leads to a lot of fat and thin shots. Therefore, for solid contact from any uneven lie, your first priority is to start in balance by making the recommended set up adjustments.

the slope of the hill, with your left shoulder higher than your right.

■ In the case of a severe uphill slope, the low point of your swing changes dramatically so it's important to level your hips as much as possible. In the process, since you open your stance, the ball in effect moves forward but when you tilt your shoulders to match the hill, the ball, in relation to your body, moves backward. The two adjustments cancel each other out and your ball is played from the middle of your stance.

Summary

Open your stance until your hips are level and adjust the position of the ball to the middle of your stance. Flare your left foot and tilt your shoulders to match the slope, right shoulder lower than left. As with all uneven lies, to maintain balance make a smooth three-quarter swing.

Downhill lies

The technique for the downhill lie is the opposite to that of the uphill lie. Since your right foot is above your left foot, it is difficult to transfer your weight up the slope to your right side during your backswing, and even harder to stay behind the ball on your downswing since the hill pulls you forward toward the target. To compensate, anchor your weight on your left foot and leave it there throughout your swing.

1   When you sole your club the slope decreases its loft so choke down on your club to reduce the

distance it produces. Aim to the left of the target and draw your right foot back until your hips are level. This not only provides you with stability but also squares your shoulders to the target line.

2   Tilt your shoulders so they match the slope of the hill and position the ball in the middle of your stance to place it at the bottom of your arc. Your left foot should be toed in to prevent you from sliding down the slope.

3   With your weight firmly anchored in your left hip, make a good upper body turn away from the ball using your left hip as the axis all the way through your swing. The major error here is to try and lift the ball into the air. This is a sure way to top the ball, so take special care to swing down the hill, letting your club head follow the contour of the slope.

Summary

Choose a more lofted club and choke down. Close your stance to level your hips, adjusting the ball to the middle of your stance. Tilt your shoulders to match the slope, left shoulder lower than right. Make a three-quarter motion, concentrating on keeping your balance throughout the swing.

Note on loft

There are four degrees of loft between each of your irons, and each degree accounts for about two-and-a-half yards of distance. Therefore, depending on how much a slope adds to the club's loft (uphill) or decreases the loft (downhill), slopes can dramatically affect the distance and trajectory of your shots.

Downhill lies are a challenge not only to your physical skills but to your mental skills as well. Many golfers try to help the ball into the air from a downhill lie, but the key is to swing down the slope which requires you to keep the club moving down and low through impact. If you think about trying to lift the ball, you'll make a contrary motion.

Chapter ten

Learning the game

There are a number of ways to learn to play better golf. The first step is to choose a model. This involves not only copying the mannerisms and swing motion of an expert player with whom you match up well but also breaking the golf swing down into manageable parts, finding the perfect model for each and then copying that model perfectly until it becomes ingrained as a habit.

One way to do this is to take lessons where the models for every part of the swing are presented to you. Then you take your models and practice them, piece by piece, until you have built a functional golf swing. Once you've done this, it's

Golf instruction comes in a variety of formats and you'll learn most quickly when you choose the method that is right for you.

time to play the game of golf on the course and that involves knowing how to manage the course and, just as importantly, how to manage yourself.

Please remember, however, that the golf swing, no matter how well memorized, is still a creative act born out of the conditions of the moment, no two of which are ever the same. Whereas you can reduce the swing to its individual pieces, you cannot reduce the game to a science. It is an art and you are the artist.

Modeling

Human beings are experts at modeling. A young child watches closely how her mother reacts in a certain situation and copies that behavior. If the situation occurs often enough, the behavior becomes a habit. Learning is a combination of nature, the potentials we are born with, and nurture, the experiences that shape our lives. We all have the potential to play better golf; that's the nature part. The question is how well do we organize our experiences so that our learning is efficient and rapid; that's the nurture part, the part that's under your control.

Chuck Hogan in his excellent book, *Learning Golf,* outlines the modeling process as follows: first you pick a model for the piece of the swing you want to learn—it might be the grip, stance or the position of your club at the top of your swing. Then you match that model in every detail. Once you're able to match it perfectly, then you repeat your perfect match until it becomes so ingrained that you can do it automatically every time. At this point it's in your long-term memory and you can now go on to the next "piece."

Learning the game by using a series of precise models as templates is nicely augmented when you choose a golfer as a model. Linda Vollstedt, one of the most successful college coaches in the history of golf, encourages her players to use models to enhance what she feels is the common trait among champions: self confidence. Linda says, "You have to practice self confidence, so I have my players think about the qualities associated with being self confident and then practice them." Her first step is to have her players pick "a role model" because, as she points out, "they are going to have to model that behavior." Similarly she advises beginners to pick a model for their swing, but she stresses that when doing so you should realize that everyone is built differently and has a different

swing, so pick out a role model that you feel you can be like, i.e. someone with the same body type and a similar level of fitness.

When learning the fundamentals of your set up, your golf instructor can serve as a model for you to copy.

113

Finding the correct models

Few golfers get to be low handicappers without some form of professional help, especially if they start as adults. You don't need a "perfect" swing but there are a few concepts that you'll need to master if you want to improve. Without these basic concepts, golf really is a difficult game. But with good fundamentals, you can build a repeatable swing that gives you consistent results and sets you on a path toward improvement.

Taking lessons

Kinesthetic learners improve most quickly by doing drills that enhance their feel for the golf swing.

Good teachers have spent years developing the appropriate models for your golf swing but how do you find these teachers, and how do you "take" a lesson? Remember that your brain learns the imperfect just as well as the perfect so it's up to you to present it with the perfect.

Since taking a golf lesson is a completely interactive experience you'll give as much as you take in a good learning experience. You'll want to consider not only your instructor's skill level, but also if they are the type of person who shapes the lesson to fit your learning style. It's your lesson and it's up to you to let your instructor know how you want the material presented.

If you learn best by understanding the detailed elements of your golf swing you'll need an instructor who will teach you details. If you're not a detail person and are more comfortable learning the general concepts in a holistic sense, then that's how your instructor needs to structure your learning experience.

Linda Vollstedt says, "For a novice the most important thing is having the right match up with a teacher who can communicate in your learning style. Teaching style is extremely important in the beginning. When you get that right match, where the instructor teaches according to your needs, you learn very quickly."

In other words, it helps to know your own learning style, be it visual, kinesthetic or auditory. If you're primarily a visual learner, find an

Visual learners acquire most of their knowledge of golf through observation.

instructor who will show you your swing on video and can then physically demonstrate the instructions they have for your golf swing. If you're an auditory learner, find a great communicator who gives precise instructions and explains things clearly. If you're a great athlete who succeeds at most sports without instruction and you don't like complicated thoughts, stick with a teacher who can plug you in to how your swing should feel rather than wasting time with long verbal explanations and detailed video analysis. A good teacher, taking care not to miss the student's dom-inant learning mode, presents the important material in all three modes so you'll see it, hear it and feel it. It's up to you to direct your instructor in this regard.

To be a good learner, first you should know some things about your own personality and then try to match the instructor to meet your needs. When you find a teacher whose personality and communication style is compatible with your own you'll improve at a much faster rate. Thus, how to find a compatible instructor is an impor-tant part of learning to play better golf.

Choosing an instructor

As with any other choice of professional, you'll want to be sure your instructor is well qualified. Verifying their membership of a professional organization is a good place to start. The Ladies Professional Golfers Association (LPGA) or The Professional Golfers Association of America (PGA) are the most highly respected organizations that certify instructors. They each require an apprenticeship for their members and oblige members to continue their education throughout their careers. Like other professional organizations, they have standards their members must fulfill and ethics they must uphold. There are some newer organizations but, so far, their standards are not comparable to the LPGA and PGA. You can call these organizations for verification of your instructor's status or ask them to recommend an instructor in your area.

Interviewing your teacher

Once you verify your teacher's professional status, ask them, or the person scheduling their lessons, about their experience level. How many years have they been giving lessons? How often do they teach? Do they have experience teaching a student at your level? Do they have a certain

method of instruction? Do they teach women on a regular basis? Did they plug into your dominant learning mode?

If you're satisfied with your instructor's qualifications, schedule one lesson. Once you get to know your instructor, you may want to schedule a series of lessons. Before you do, though, interview your instructor a little more. Ask what their plan would be for improving your swing over the course of the series. Set some goals together and have the instructor outline the steps you'll take together and what you'll need to do on your own to make significant improvement.

Lesson formats: what to expect

Golf instruction comes in all shapes and sizes. The most common format is an individual lesson, where you and your instructor go to the driving range to work on your swing. The first step should be an interview where your instructor finds out about you and your game. Then you'll be asked to hit a few balls so your instructor can

Repeating the correct motion with the help of a training aid can help you to see and feel how your golf club should work. Your golf instructor can help you choose the correct training aids and make sure you're using them properly.

get an idea of your natural tendencies: how you hold the club, how you arrange your body in relationship to the ball and target and the motion of your swing.

Be a good learner

Once your instructor has evaluated your swing, you'll both know what changes you need to make to improve. There may be two or three problems that are causing you trouble but your goal is to prioritize and then fix one problem at a time. While you're working on these changes, don't judge your performance based on where the ball

goes, but on whether or not you executed the correction motion. This attention to task performance is the hallmark of a good learner. For example, if you're working on your take away, focus solely on that and your instructor's rating of how well you performed that particular task—don't be controlled by the ball flight. You can see how your brain could get confused. Let's say you make a perfect take away but hit a bad shot. Your teacher says, "Excellent, that's just what we're looking for," evaluating your take away. You say, "What an awful shot." Your brain says, "Well, which is it? Is it good or bad?" And a confused learner is a bad learner.

Linda Vollstedt, Head Coach of Arizona State University Women's Golf Team, says, "As the skills and mechanics get to the point where you have a better understanding of the movement of the golf swing (the importance of rhythm, balance and timing), then you can get on the golf course and learn how to play golf.

"Learning golf is not just about standing on the driving range hitting golf balls; you need to get out on the golf course and learn to play golf. Many teachers don't teach how to play golf; they teach how to 'swing golf.' But my teaching philosophy is the opposite of most. I feel most teaching should be done on the golf course, even with beginners. Especially when someone has learned to swing the golf club and hit the ball. I can teach more in 30 minutes on the golf course than I can in three days on the driving range."

Choosing an instructor *continued*

Group lessons

Many resorts, clubs and driving ranges offer clinics on different aspects of the game. One session may be dedicated to putting and another to bunker play. Usually the sessions last for an hour or two. Clinics start with a presentation from the teacher on the chosen topic after which you'll work on these skills. Depending on the size of the group, you'll have varying amounts of individual attention. This is a good way for beginners to get a taste for instruction without a big investment of time or money. It's also a good idea for intermediate golfers who need to brush up on their fundamentals. Group lessons are probably a

Arranging a group lesson for yourself and some friends can be a comfortable way to get started with golf instruction.

waste of time for the good player.

If you don't know of a clinic held in your area, it's easy to arrange one for your own group of friends or business associates. First, find out how many participants you'll have and what part of the game your group would like to learn. Then contact your golf professional and arrange the time, date and price structure. Many women find this is an excellent way to get started with instruction, because they are among friends and the program is tailored specifically to their requests.

Short game lessons

Be sure to dedicate at least an equal amount of your lesson to your short game, especially putting, since putting alone accounts for more than 40 percent of your game. If distance isn't your strong suit, a good short game can be a great equalizer. Remember that a two-foot putt counts for just as much on your score card as a 250-yard drive. So either schedule separate short game lessons or divide your lesson time between the full swing and the short game.

Playing lessons

You can have your pro take you on the course for what's known as a playing lesson. The objective here is not to work on your mechanics but your course management skills, and such things as shot selection and how to handle adversity. To do this efficiently, you won't play each shot in succession as you do with your friends, but you'll go to different "situations" and learn to manage your way around the course based on your current golf skills. It is impossible to learn to play golf on a driving range so, once you have some basics, be sure your golf pro takes you on the course and teaches you the essence of the game of golf.

1   If you're serious about lowering your handicap, be sure to dedicate at least an equal portion of your lesson time and practice to your short game skills.

2   When you take playing lessons, you will learn strategy and course management techniques.

Golf schools

When choosing a golf school be sure to check not only the package price but also make a careful inquiry as to the following:

■ Find out who actually does the teaching. Is there a "big name" associated with the school? Determine to what extent that person participates in the school you plan to attend.

■ Find out the teacher-student ratio; it should be at least four to one if you are going to get enough individual attention.

■ Ask about the format of the school: how much time is dedicated to the short game, on-course instruction, etc?

■ Ask if your progress is video-taped and if they give you the tape to take home to work from.

At the Academy of Golf at PGA National, you will find Director Mike Adams involved in every school.

The Players School at PGA National features course management and mental strategy instruction from Dr. T.J. Tomasi.

Course management and strategy schools

If you are satisfied with your ball striking but need help with your playing ability you can go to a school specifically designed to enhance these skills. Like an in-depth and extended playing lesson, you'll learn how to handle the inner game of golf. Golf is a thinking person's game and schools like this can teach you how to manage your game, your shot selections and your emotions once you get to the course.

Summary

Regardless of what format you choose for instruction, make sure you don't mix yourself up with too many different theories. Carefully select your teacher and then stick with that person. Expect to learn golf at a similar rate to which you learned other sports. If this is your first attempt at a sport, relate the learning process to other skills you've acquired: playing the piano, trigonometry, chess, gardening. Regardless of the skill and unless you're a prodigy, learning something new is a process that requires instruction, a dedication to practice and the exercise of your new skills on the course. Golf is no different and you'll get out of it what you put into it.

PGA
National

At the Academy of Golf at PGA National, the Director, Mike Adams, fully participates in every school. The teacher-student ratio, which includes Mike Adams and often Dr. T.J. Tomasi, is generally three to one. The golf school is a comprehensive three-day program, during which students work on all basic elements of the game: full swing, putting, chipping, pitching, side-hill and awkward lies, fairway and green side bunkers, and also on-course instruction. A mental strategy program for learning and playing is also given. A student's full-swing instruction with Mike Adams is recorded on their take-home video as is a program for improvement which Mike goes over with them personally.

Coach Linda Vollstedt

Practice

An important part of learning

Once you've taken a lesson you've got to practice what you learned until it becomes a habit. It's been said many times before but it bears repeating that practice does not make perfect, it makes permanent. Only perfect practice makes perfect. This means that it's up to you to make your practice as perfect as you can by choosing the correct models and then repeating the perfect match over and over again until you've got it. Chuck Hogan says that to make a habit you must practice at least 60 perfect repetitions a day for 21 consecutive days.

Learning to play better golf is a process just like any other skill you've learned. And to help you along your journey we've solicited the advice of one of golf's most respected coaches. In 1996, coach Linda Vollstedt led Arizona State University Women's Golf Team to its fifth NCAA Championship of the decade and its fourth title in as many years, both record-breaking statistics. In fact, Coach Vollstedt has received almost every coaching honor available and has produced some of the leading stars on the LPGA Tour.

If you've been stuck with a high handicap for a number of years, Linda offers the following plan for lowering your scores. "First," she says, "have your equipment checked. See a good club fitter and make sure you're swinging a club that helps you hit the ball your best." Second, she recommends playing lessons. "You need a teacher who is willing to take you on the course, find out how you're thinking, and understand how you actually play golf." Third, she stresses improving your short game through practice, lessons and proper equipment, which involves her fourth point, the specific clubs you choose to put in your bag. "Equipment is so important. Understand what a variety of wedges can do and have at least two in your bag, preferably three." Regarding equipment, Coach Vollstedt feels that "most women should be playing with a seven and a nine wood and get rid of their three and four iron."

If you're serious about your playing ability, whether you're 16 or 60, a beginner or advanced,

In 1996, Arizona State Women's Golf Coach Linda Vollstedt led her team to a record-breaking fifth NCAA Championship Title of the decade.

you can nurture the qualities in yourself that Coach Vollstedt looks for in a recruit seeking to join her highly successful program. "I'm looking for that kid who's driven, someone who has a really good attitude and the qualities that are going to help them be successful, like self confidence. Mostly I want to watch how they handle themselves." What she doesn't want is a person who gets upset about every small mistake. For example, she would not recruit someone who showed their frustration by throwing their clubs?

After years observing her elite athletes Coach Vollstedt picked out the traits these players had in common when playing their best. "They have a good understanding of who they are and how they operate, they play within themselves, they are in control of their emotions, and their patterns are consistent." So in a fast-paced person that pattern should remain consistent on the course, and a comparable pattern should be evident in a slow-paced person.

Coach Vollstedt says, "When a player gets out of her rhythm her golf score goes up. When I see someone play poorly I ask myself, 'How are they different?' and I ask them, 'When you're playing really well, what's it like?' and 'When you're playing really poorly, what's it like?' I want them to think about it, and realize what happens when they're playing really well, and I try to get those patterns to be consistent."

You can be your own coach and watch for changes like this in your own personality when you're playing. Also, you can follow the other coaching techniques Linda works on with her players. "I'm always trying to have everything in their favor. I tell my players how to put the odds in their favor: think positively, one shot at a time, and don't complain about the things you can't change. If the wind is blowing, have the attitude that says, 'I'm a good wind player and other people are going to get frustrated but I'm not going to let that happen to me,' so you're always playing the odds so that when the opportunity comes up for you to have a spectacular round, the odds are going to increase that it's going to happen. I talk to my players a lot about patience, a word we use a lot, but what does it mean? To me, patience just means being in a position for something good to happen."

Advice for
girls' junior programs

Coach Vollstedt feels that a successful junior program for girls must be structured so that girls can enjoy themselves while they learn. "It's got to be fun for girls. You are going to have a very small percentage of young females who, in spite of everything else that's going on around them, are going to jump out of the pack and make it, probably half of one percent. And that's your Brandie Burtons, Michelle McGanns, Dottie Mochries, Nancy Lopezes. They are destined to be great golfers. Nothing is going to get in their way."

If you have a junior interested in becoming a champion keep in mind a key factor that Linda Vollstedt has observed in her years of coaching: "Most really good players had someone extremely influential in their life; someone who helped them learn to play golf and inspired them to play golf, most often their father or a father figure that got them started." Although she feels that lessons are very important, inspiration is an even greater factor.

The power of imagery

Once you've learned to swing the club, it's time to learn how to use your power to create images in your mind. They direct motor responses, and are a representation of reality by your brain. Your senses are image-makers. Among others, you have visual images, kinesthetic images, and auditory images. The brain synthesizes these images into a fine-tuned experience and then it acts on it, turning it into motor behavior. For each shot, therefore, you feel the wind, hear the wind, see the flag blowing, and your brain automatically makes a calculation as to the effect the wind will have on your shot. These images are then translated into movements designed to satisfy the plan that you have made. So your arms swing, and your body turns, all at a speed and a pace that will get the ball to target.

Chapter eleven

Course design and strategy

One of golf's most compelling features is its playing field. Unlike the uniform boundaries of a soccer field or the rigid dimensions of a tennis court, golf courses come in an endless array of shapes and sizes. At their finest, they are truly a work of art, sculpted by the architect and the whims of nature, to offer golfers a field of play unrivaled in any other sport.

A course can be short in distance and tightly bounded by trees and water, or long and open with heavy rough and treacherous greens. Depending on the location, be it seaside, moun-

The Champion Course at PGA National is the annual host of the Senior PGA Championship. To beat the "champ," you'll need to conquer its many challenges, such as sand, water, trees, rough and wind.

tainous or barren desert, each course offers special situations that challenge you to adapt your skills and strategies to the design features built in by the architect. To conquer the inevitable variations you'll face, you need to understand the features that all golf courses have in common.

The concept of par

A championship course features 18 different holes consisting of a mixture of par threes, par fours and par fives, so named for the number of times it takes an expert to hit the ball from the teeing ground into the hole.

Regulation par

Although there are many ways to "make par" the standard is as follows.

■ **On par threes**, the shortest distance holes, you'll hit your ball from the tee to the green in one shot.

■ **On par fours**, the intermediate distance holes, you'll hit your tee shot to the ideal landing area in the fairway and from there hit your "approach shot" on to the green.

■ **On par fives**, the longest holes on the course, you'll hit your tee shot and your second shot to the ideal landing areas in the fairway, then hit

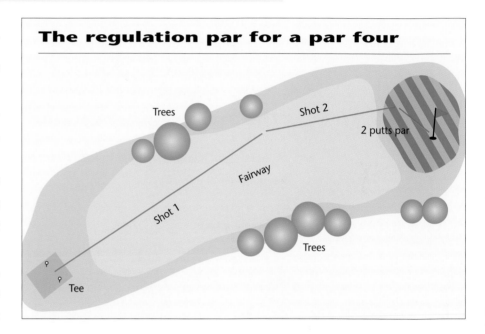

The regulation par for a par four

Trees
Shot 2
2 putts par
Fairway
Shot 1
Trees
Tee

Design without you in mind

In the past, golf courses were often an intimidating place for women because they were typically designed with two considerations: the professional male golfer and the amateur male golfer. The "ladies" tees were generally an afterthought to course design, if they existed at all. Often these tees were just a few yards ahead of the men's tees, a totally insignificant distance adjustment. When ladies' tees were finally added to courses, they did provide distance adjustments, but often these tees were placed "off to the side" of a hole, forcing women to play from odd angles. Modern-day course architect Rees Jones says, "In the past, forward tees weren't given any thought or as much as they are today so that even if the distance was adjusted, the angle would create an obstacle."

Fortunately, the world of golf course design has changed dramatically and today architects give special attention to the strategic location of each tee box. In fact, even the terminology has changed. Jan Beljan of Fazio Golf Course Designers echoes the modern sentiments of her fellow golf course designers: "We don't call them 'ladies' tees' anymore because we have our tees assigned as gender neutral and age neutral." Today's golf courses feature the forward, middle and back tees and golfers are encouraged to choose the tee most appropriate to the distance they hit the ball and their current playing ability. Most newer courses are built with four and five sets of tees so golfers of all levels have an appropriate, yet challenging, golf course.

On a par four, you will make a par in "regulation" when you hit your tee shot onto the fairway, your approach shot onto the green, and take two putts to get the ball in the hole.

The concept of par *continued*

your approach shot on to the green. Once you reach each green, you are allotted two putts to make your score equal to par.

These examples are what's know as a "regulation par," but since golf is a game where mis-hits are common, even the world's best players sometimes struggle to make par in "regulation," if at all.

The "non-regulation par"

You can still make par even though your tee shot misses the fairway or your approach shot

misses the green. For example, on a par four, you might hit your ball into the trees and make a miraculous "recovery shot" out of the woods but land just short of the green. From there, you could make what's known as an "up and down" by hitting a difficult pitch shot from heavy rough to within six feet of the hole and sinking the putt. Although not a "regulation" par, you've still made par and on the score card what counts is not "how" but "how many."

At other times, your score will be more than par or "over par" and sometimes when you're firing on all cylinders, you'll get the ball in the hole in fewer strokes than par or "under par."

When you take one stroke more than par, you've made what's known as a bogey; two strokes more than par is a double bogey. Triple and quadruple bogeys follow, and after that no one's much interested in talking about their score, to say nothing about writing it down. If you take one stroke less than par, you've made a birdie, two strokes less is an eagle, three less is a double eagle. If your tee shot goes in the hole that's known as a hole-in-one. There's nothing normal about a hole-in-one but, when it happens, it's almost always on a par three. In this case you've actually made an eagle (two shots under the par).

There's an endless variety of ways to make a non-regulation par. In this example, your tee shots finds the trees, your recovery shot is short of the green, your third shot lands close to the hole and you one putt for par.

The non-regulation par

Shot 3
Shot 4
Green
Shot 2
Trees
Shot 1
Trees
Fairway
Tee box

Guidelines for course management

Rees Jones says, "Definition is important in golf course design today. If an architect designs a hole to help the golfer determine what to do, then the golfer has a better chance of hitting the proper shot and achieving their goal." So when you arrive at the tee box take a few moments to identify the shape of the hole and what the architect had in mind. Each hole has a route from the tee to the green, which is indicated by the fairway, but rarely is it a straight line. Like chess, golf is a game of strategy and you'll need to think a move or two ahead to make a successful plan of attack.

If you're at a new course and the layout of the hole isn't clear from the tee, be sure to look at the map of the hole on your score card or on a placard that's often by the tee box as you drive up to the hole. Or ask one of your playing partners, who knows the course, to give you an idea what's out there.

Know thyself

A successful strategy for playing golf involves knowing your strengths and weaknesses and matching them to the demands of the golf course. Keep an honest and up-to-date inventory of your current skills and play to your strengths when you get to the course. The more you know about your capabilities the better you can adapt to the demands of the course.

For example, if you're a great fairway wood player but not so great with the driver, use your three or five wood off the tee when you absolutely have to hit the fairway. If you're a good pitcher of the ball but not a good bunker player, you might play short of a deep green side bunker, then pitch your ball safely onto the green. We're not advocating that you be content with your weakness but that you play to your current strengths. Make a note of your weaknesses and then give them special attention on the practice tee. Your strategy is simple: to improve your game, keep your strengths up to date and to focus on eliminating your weaknesses.

As you approach the teeing ground, you should check the map of the hole, which is usually located by the back tees.

When faced with difficult bunkers surrounding a green, you should evaluate your current skill level and plan your strategy accordingly.

127

Guidelines for course management *continued*

Tee shot strategy

Once you've evaluated the layout of the hole, be sure to look at your options from both sides of the tee. Sometimes, a short walk to the other side of the tee gives you a better angle to your target. A good rule of thumb is to tee up on the side of trouble but aim away from it. If you're a slicer of the golf ball, tee the ball on the right side and aim down the left side of the fairway. If you hit it straight, you're in good shape; if you slice it, the worst result may be that you land in the right rough. The opposite is true for a hooker of the ball.

However, remember that "trouble" is relative to the way you hit the ball. If you tend to mis-hit to the right, you'll be more concerned about the fairway bunker on the right than the large pond on the left. But even if you rarely hit the ball straight, never aim your ball at the trouble and expect it to curve back to safety.

In general, the idea is to always play away from the trouble. What do you do when there's big trouble on both sides of the fairway? Choose a club you know is going to get you on the fairway even if it's a long hole and you have to hit a five iron. You may not be able to reach the green in regulation but you'll avoid penalty strokes and if you follow your tee shot with a couple of solid shots, you'll be close enough to the green to rely on your short game to keep your score down.

Although the same teeing ground is shown in both pictures, each side of the tee offers a different perspective of the hole. A golfer whose ball flight usually curves from right to left has a better angle from the left side of the tee (1), but from the right side of the tee (2) her margin for error is much smaller due to the proximity of the trees on the right.

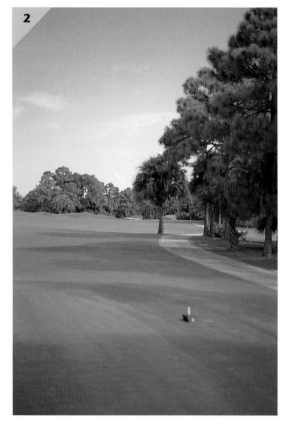

Playing a course poorly designed for women

From the teeing ground, a dangerous situation occurs when the tee box points away from the ideal landing area. Sometimes it's the tee markers that point toward the trouble rather than the fairway. If you make it a habit to set up square to the direction of the tee, you may be aiming your ball into trouble.

From the forward tees this problem occurs most frequently. Although modern architects are making real improvements, many times the forward tees are severely misaligned simply because they were an after-thought to course design. This problem is most prevalent on older courses where the "ladies' tees" were added years after the course was built, often without guidance from the original architect.

Aiming correctly is a difficult task in golf and a misaligned tee compounds the problem. Since your brain converts all visual images into geometric shapes, the straight, orderly line formed by the tee markers is very attractive.

You'll need to train yourself to ignore these lines when they aim into trouble and draw some target lines of your own.

It's important to identify the trouble tees on your course. To do so, approach the tee box from

Aiming correctly from a misaligned tee

Trees

Men's tee

Fairway

Good target line

Pro's tee

Women's tee

Water hazard

Trees

Are odd angles a maintenance problem?

If a forward tee box is set just slightly to the side of the hole it shouldn't create too much of a problem for you unless it's not being maintained correctly. Architect Alice Dye deliberately places many forward tees to the side so that they can be elevated in the same way as other tees, but she says, "We do build them so they're pointing in the correct direction." However, she cautions that "the maintenance people need to cut these tees at an angle that points to the fairway and set the markers in the same direction." If your tees sit to the side of the fairway, be sure that the proper maintenance procedures are followed so that the visual distortion is eliminated. Jan Beljan of Fazio Design adds that if the angle is "so bad, it would behove the golfers who play from this tee to voice their opinion and find out if there are funds available to create some new tees." We suggest a meeting with the superintendent to address the problem of any incorrectly placed tee markers.

Playing a course poorly designed for women *continued*

behind. This gives you the most accurate perspective on where the tee markers are aligned. If you notice the line of the tee is pointing away from the fairway, be especially careful in picking your target. On these holes, as with all your shots, concentrate on a pre-shot routine that's dedicated to good aim and alignment. See page 31 for the details of pre-shot routines.

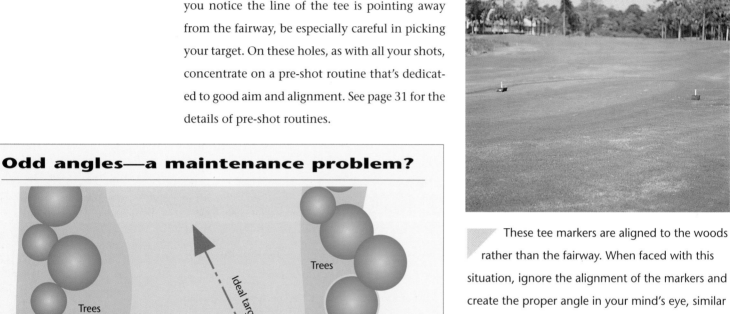

These tee markers are aligned to the woods rather than the fairway. When faced with this situation, ignore the alignment of the markers and create the proper angle in your mind's eye, similar to the angle at which this photo was taken.

Odd angles—a maintenance problem?

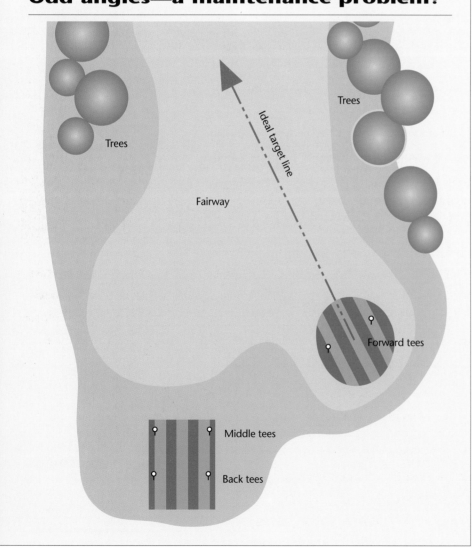

Trees

Trees

Ideal target line

Fairway

Forward tees

Middle tees

Back tees

When you can't reach the green in regulation

Occasionally the total yardage of the hole exceeds your ability to reach the green in regulation. When this happens don't use your driver off the tee if you're not an accurate driver to begin with. For example, if you're faced with a long par four that's beyond your ability to reach the green in two shots, choose a club off the tee that you can confidently hit into the fairway. Since the distance puts you at a disadvantage before you even start the hole you don't need to complicate matters by hitting an errant driver into the trees. Once you're safely in play off the tee, you're ready for your approach to the green.

Approach shots

On par fours and fives your attempt at hitting your ball onto the green is called your "approach" shot. The first piece of information you need to make a good approach is the yardage to the pin. Most courses have markers or colored disks in the center of the fairway, indicating 100 (red), 150 (white) and 200 (blue) yards to the center of the green. You may also find yardage markings on the cart paths, sprinkler heads or posts on the sides of the fairway that indicate 150 yards. Check to find out how the course is marked and if the yardage is measured to the front or center of the green (it's usually to the center).

Once you have your yardage to the center of the green, locate the pin in relation to the center of the green. Most greens are at least 30 yards deep so if the pin is in the back of the green, you need to add about 10 yards to your distance; if it's in the front of the green, you need to subtract about 10 yards. Once you know the yardage, take into consideration how conditions, such as wind and elevation, will affect your ball flight.

Wind

If you're playing in windy conditions, you need to determine exactly how much distance it will effectively add to or subtract from your shot. You can ignore anything less than five miles per hour but if it's blowing more than that, you'll need to adjust your club selection. You won't have a scientific way to measure the strength of the wind, but as a golfer you'll learn to use the measuring devices available to you.

■ For example, if your shirt sleeves are fluttering in the breeze and your hair is blowing about, you probably have more than a five-mile-per-hour wind.

■ Also, look at the clouds to see how quickly they're moving, as well as the flagstick to see if it's waving and in what direction.

■ If the shot you're planning will get above the tree-tops, pay close attention to the amount and direction in which they are moving.

Once you've made your analysis, adjust your club selection as follows: for every five to ten miles per hour of wind, add one club if you're hitting into the wind, and subtract one if it's behind you.

A side wind is not a helping wind because for most of its journey, your ball is fighting the wind. It's only at its apex when it blows your ball sideways that the wind can be considered helpful. You adjust for a side wind, using about two-thirds of what you would adjust for a head wind of the same speed—for example, a side wind of nine miles per hour is treated as a head wind of six miles per hour.

Lie and elevation

First, you must take your lie into consideration.

■ From the rough, if the grass is moving in the same direction as you intend to hit your ball, it causes the ball to jump off the club face so you can figure your ball will travel a greater distance.

Most courses feature markers or colored disks in the fairway which indicate your yardage to the green.

The key to playing in the wind is to hit the ball solidly. So the old saw, "when it's breezy, swing easy," is a good guide. Since you've already compensated for the wind by adding a club, avoid the temptation to swing "hard" in a head wind. If you do, the chances are that you'll mis-hit your ball and the wind will have an even greater effect. Be confident that you have the right club and make "solid contact" your objective.

In a side wind, most players over-estimate its force and aim off the green expecting the wind to blow it back on. As you learned in Tee Strategy, never aim where a straight shot will get you into trouble, or, in golf lingo, don't "give the green away." You should favor one side or another, but never aim off the green as a compensation for a side wind.

In windy conditions, tee your ball as you normally would and keep your ball position the same. Unless you're an expert player, making variations to your set up often contributes to mis-hits.

Approach shots *continued*

■ If the grass is against you, it slows down the club, robbing you of distance, so take one more club.

You should also adjust your club selection depending on how much the green is below or above you. The guideline is that for every 30 feet of elevation, add (uphill) or subtract (downhill) 10 yards.

Pin placement

The location of the pin has a major influence on the type of shot you should play and there are many times during each round where you should not be aiming directly at the flag. Knowing when to attack and when to play safe is the hallmark of a good player.

Tucked pin

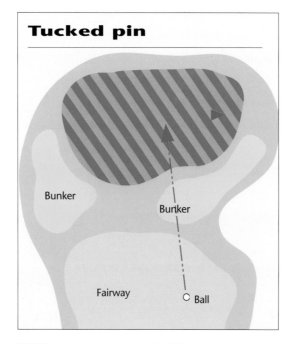

When the pin is "tucked" behind a hazard as shown here, you should always be sure to play to the safe part of the green.

Tucked pins

In golf lingo, a flagstick that is set behind a bunker or a water hazard just a short distance from the edge of the green is said to be "tucked." In this situation, it's difficult to get your ball close to the hole on your approach shot unless you know how to fade and draw the ball on command. Even expert golfers allow some margin for error for these difficult shots. If the pin is tucked left, and you can reliably draw the ball, aim at the center of the green and let the ball curve to the left, close to the pin. This way, if you happen to hit it straight, you're still in the middle of the green.

The cardinal sin in this situation is aiming straight at the flagstick. Unless your shot is perfect,

Front, middle and back pins

When using the red, yellow and green lights method, remember not to confuse this mental strategy with the actual colors of the flags. Many courses feature different flag colors to indicate whether the pin is in the front, middle or back of the green. Each course is different, but often you'll see red flags for front pins, white flags for middle pins and blue flags for back pins. These colors are often chosen because they have a loose correlation to the yardage disks in the fairway and the traditional colors of the tee markers. Thus red indicates short distance, white—medium, and blue—long distance. Before you play, be sure to ask about the color coding and don't confuse it with your red, yellow and green lights strategy.

your margin for error is too small—which is why it's called a "sucker pin." A mis-hit aimed directly at a tucked pin usually winds up in the bunker or rough with very little green between your ball and the hole. This is called "short siding" yourself because you have a short amount of green on which to stop your ball. So when the pin is tucked, the smart player, depending on their strengths and weaknesses, aims to the middle or safe side of the green.

Red, yellow and green lights

A good way to identify the type of pin you're dealing with is to label it in your mind by colors.

- Red light = don't go for it.
- Yellow light = proceed with caution.
- Green light = go for it.

Here's how it works. Evaluate the location of the pin based on the conditions. If a pin is protected by two conditions, such as a bunker, with a strong side wind that will blow your ball toward the bunker, then that's definitely a red light pin. If so stop aiming at the flag and select a

different part of the green as your target.

If the pin is protected by only one condition, such as a bunker, then you can aim closer to it, but proceed with caution by giving yourself about a 10- to 15-foot margin of error on the safe side of the pin (the side the bunker is not on). When there is no trouble surrounding the pin, or the pin's in the middle, go right at this green light situation.

Obviously, pin accessibility depends on your talent level so once again you need to compile a realistic catalogue of your strengths and weaknesses.

When the flagstick is protected by one condition, such as a bunker in this instance, use the "yellow light" strategy.

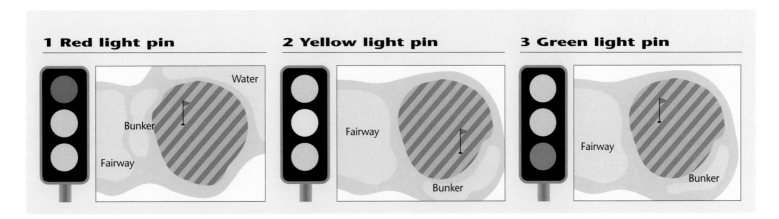

1 Red light pin

Water

Bunker

Fairway

2 Yellow light pin

Fairway

Bunker

3 Green light pin

Fairway

Bunker

Putting it all together

Beginners are often con-fused by the terms "more club" and "less club" and there's a good reason for their confusion. Irons are numbered one through nine and then PW for the pitch-ing wedge (effectively your 10 iron), and SW for the sand wedge (your 11 iron). The one iron has the longest shaft and the least amount of loft, the combination that should produce the longest, lowest ball flight of all irons. As the numbers increase, the shaft shortens and the loft increases, producing pro-gressively shorter and more lofted ball flights.

When told to take more club, a beginner often reach-es for a club with a higher number, say an eight or a nine iron. Although their logic is good, they've made the wrong choice. More club and less club refer to the distance the club can produce, not their numbers. So when you hear you need "more club," ignore the numbers and reach for the club with the next longest shaft, the one whose num-ber is one less.

To decide what shot to play, go through all your variables, adding and subtracting a club from the initial yardage, so you're sure you have the right club. Although it may seem a little compli-cated at first, before you know it, you'll be able to make these calculations in a few seconds. If you do this for every shot you hit, in a short time these adjustments become second nature.

Selecting the correct club

It's important to know how far you hit each of your clubs. There's about four degrees' loft between each of your irons, and since each degree represents about two-and-a-half yards, there is approximately 10 yards difference man-ufactured into each of your irons. Pick one club, say an eight iron, and figure out how far your average eight iron carries in the air. Go to the range and hit a bunch of eight irons and watch where they land. Keep track of how far your eight iron goes on the course—actually pace it off. Once you know the distance it goes on the fly, use this as a benchmark, adding and sub-tracting 10 yards, for the rest of your irons. For example, if your eight iron goes on average 120

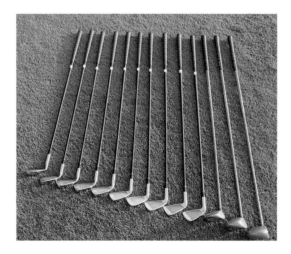

yards, then your seven iron flies 130, and your nine iron goes 110 yards.

■ **Calculation example:** you're 120 yards from the center of the green. You know you're hitting into the wind because your shirt sleeves are blow-ing about, the flag is blowing toward you, and the tree-tops are bending away from the green. You automatically add ten yards for the wind so now your distance is 130 yards. However, the green is about 30 feet below you, effectively shortening the distance by 10 yards, so you adjust back to 120 yards. Since the pin is in the back of the green, you add another 10 yards and arrive at an adjusted distance of 130 yards. Now pick the club that consistently travels 130 yards and make your normal swing.

Note: sometimes the 10-yard progression doesn't hold true as the shafts get longer. Be sure to check your long irons because, if you have a slow swing speed, you may hit all your long irons the same distance. In this case, replace your long irons with utility woods, a move you should probably make anyway.

The terms "more club" and "less club" correspond to the length of the shaft of the club, and the distance the club produces rather than the number on the club. If you are confused by these terms, see the sidebar for details.

How to play par threes, fours and fives

Par threes

According to guidelines listed in The Rules of Golf, par threes can be up to 210 yards in distance from the women's tees. Usually, there are four par threes on an 18-hole course, and often you'll find that each is a different distance which gives you an opportunity to use a variety of clubs. However, because the distance is short, don't necessarily assume the hole is easy. Par threes provide some of the game's great challenges.

Strategy

Par threes are usually defended by more bunkers than other greens so be sure to evaluate your bunker skills when making your plan. If you have a yellow light pin, guarded by a bunker, but your sand play needs work, aim your ball to a part of the green unprotected by bunkers. If the bunkers are in the front of the green, take an extra club and plan to land your ball on the back of the green. This way, you'll be sure to carry the bunkers, and if you miss the green, you won't be in the sand.

Par fours

Guidelines in The Rules of Golf specify that par fours measure between 211 and 400 yards in length for women. Once again, you'll find short, medium and long par fours over the course of 18 holes.

Architects guard par fours with length and hazards. Therefore, on a well-designed short hole with the challenge of length removed, you can be sure that trouble awaits even if you can't see it. Our advice here is to think carefully before you choose to hit a driver. But don't take too little club off the tee and leave yourself a long approach shot because short holes usually feature small greens built to accept short-iron shots. Small greens need to be approached with higher shots allowing the ball to land softly and stop quickly and this requires the loft of a shorter iron.

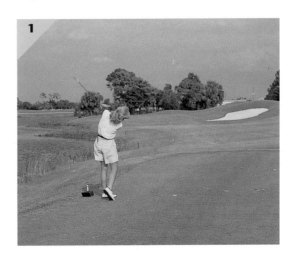

1 Evaluate your strengths and weaknesses when choosing the right club to hit on a par three.

2 A well-placed drive can put you in position to take your approach shot right at the flag.

Be sure to tee the ball at the proper height. A driver should be teed so that half of the ball is above its top edge at address. Irons should be teed rather close to the ground. A good measurement is to tee your ball so that only the thin end of a tee fits between your ball and the ground. If you tee your irons too high, you run the risk of hitting the ball high on the club face. And because you've missed the sweet spot, your shot won't go as far as you planned. When you tee your woods (other than your driver) too high, you could literally skim right under the ball and contact the top of the club head rather than the face, producing a very high short shot known as a "pop up."

How to play par threes, fours and fives *continued*

If possible, observe the location of the flag so you can favor the side of the fairway and position your tee shot to give you the best angle for your approach shot. On a dog-leg hole, so named for its resemblance to the shape of a dog's hind leg, be especially careful to hit the correct side of the fairway. On a dog leg that bends from left to right, for example, you might not have a clear shot to the green if you land your ball on the right side of the fairway, so your plan should be to position your ball on the left side of the fairway.

When the par four requires a long approach shot, most of the trouble will be to the left and right, to catch off-line shots, but thankfully long par fours also feature large greens which are receptive to longer shots, so take plenty of club

On a dog-leg that bends from left to right, try to position your tee shot on the left side of the fairway where you will usually find less trouble and have a better angle to the green.

and make a smooth swing. If you have a favorite "straight" club (say, a seven or five wood) use it to stay out of trouble.

When you're faced with a really long par four that's out of your range in "regulation," treat it as a par five and lay up to your strength. For example, if you struggle with 30-yard pitch shots and feel more comfortable with a full shot from about 100 yards, don't hit a driver and three wood if that puts you an awkward 30 yards from the green. Use your three wood from the tee, and then, say, your seven wood so you're left with a full shot of 100 yards. This way you can hit an approach shot of which you feel more comfortable. The logic of proper course management is: since you can't reach the hole in two, choose more accurate clubs for your first and second shots and then have a shot to the green that gives you the opportunity to knock your ball close to the hole. The key on the long par fours is to avoid the score-wrecking big number that inevitably occurs when trying to reach every par four in two because you're "supposed to."

Par fives

Par fives, according to The Rules of Golf guidelines, are 401 to 575 yards for women. A distance in excess of 576 yards is considered a par six for women players.

Theoretically they're the hardest holes because they're the longest, forcing amateurs to take the most swings and thereby increasing the odds of a mistake. But for those who hit the ball long and straight, par fives can be the easiest holes.

Architects design trouble on par fives to test long hitters who can reach the green in two shots rather than three. If you go for a par five in two, trouble almost certainly awaits a mis-hit or mis-directed long shot to the green. If you play the hole conservatively in the standard three shots, once again, make sure you lay up to your strengths. Keep "the odds" of not making a mistake in your favor by making good club selections.

Hazards, especially water, often guard the entrances to par fives. They are intended to catch the mis-hits of the long hitter who goes for the green in two, but sometimes they cause problems for those who choose the three-shot route. To avoid this, once again be sure you choose the right club for your second shot lay-up. The worst mistake you can make on a par five is to lay up into the water; always remember that it's much better to be 10 yards too short than one yard too long. And always lay-up to a level lie; it's more important to have level footing than it is to be 10 yards closer to the green, especially if you have to carry your approach shot over water.

You must keep your concentration at a high level on par fives since they require the most shots and thereby increase the odds of one being a mis-hit.

Golf course architecture

The ladies' tees, now more appropriately called the forward tees, have been the topic of much discussion as the number of women golfers continues to increase. Appropriate changes have been made on many newer courses to accommodate shorter hitters, and some older courses have done redesign work for the same purpose. But many golfers still struggle on courses that don't offer them an appropriate playing field. And some golfers have lost the basic concept of the game, the regulation par, because they've played for so many years on courses whose greens are literally out of their reach in regulation. Although no one makes par on every hole, if you've been playing for several years and don't have the ability to reach most of your greens in regulation with your good shots, you're playing a course that's too long.

The thirteenth hole at Casa de Campo is short in distance but still features plenty of challenge from the forward tees. This is a good illustration of architect Alice Dye's excellent philosophy in design for shorter hitters.

To assist you in your considerations, we spoke with some top golf course architects, so that their method of design from the forward tees would give you an idea of how a truly modern course should be arranged. Also, this section will expand your understanding about course design so that your proposal for change will be backed up by a deeper knowledge of what you want achieved.

Of the architects consulted, each said that distance was their primary consideration in their design of courses from the forward tees, but they also mentioned other factors that are relevant to placement of tee boxes based on the challenges of the golf hole. Their perspectives on design from the forward tees is offered here.

Alice Dye

Golf course architect Alice Dye, who, in partnership with her husband Pete, has created such famous layouts as TPC Sawgrass in Florida and PGA West in California, says, "Distance is the most important consideration from any tee, because the golfer has to be able to get to the green. And since distance is the most heavily weighted mark of difficulty in USGA course rating, it's our first consideration from any tee."

Alice goes on to make the point that a long hole, free of hazards, may be more difficult for shorter hitters than a shorter hole with many hazards, because the player still has to hit more shots getting to the longer hole. "We know the average lady hits the ball about 130 yards. Even if you had an above-average golfer, who hit the ball

150 yards, after two shots on a 525-yard par five she's still only traveled 300 yards." Thus after two good shots this woman still has the equivalent of a short par four (225 yards) remaining to the hole. Since each swing increases the probability of a bad shot, the more swings per hole the higher the probability becomes.

Her second objective is to "get the average woman golfer off to a good start" by letting her have a relatively clear tee shot so that, unless she hits a really bad shot, she'll have the opportunity to advance her next shot toward the green. This way, Dye says, the hole becomes manageable since the average woman with a good short game is quite capable of facing the challenges around the green. As Dye points out, "This woman can get out of the bunker or chip onto the green or make an approach shot with a short iron and play a respectable game."

However, put a lot of trouble off the tee and it's a score wrecker. "If she gets in a ditch, bunker or high rough off the tee, then the hole becomes almost unmanageable for her." In this case Alice is once again referring to the average woman who hits the ball 130 yards. Golfers at this skill level often don't have the strength to get out of the high rough or a deep fairway bunker with enough distance to get close to the green. When they're in trouble off the tee, they're forced to waste strokes to recover only to find they're still a long way from the green. Thus in a user-friendly design, both distance and position are targeted to help get the forward tee player off to a good start. Alice says, "Though our goal is to get the

woman off to a good start it doesn't mean that the hole still isn't challenging. She's got plenty of challenge left."

Rees Jones

Architect Rees Jones, who early in his career collaborated with his world-renowned father, Robert Trent Jones, has himself designed many primer courses, such as LPGA International in Florida, and The Atlantic Club in New York. He has also had the opportunity to restore many legendary Tillinghast Courses, such as Baltusrol, Quaker Ridge and Pinehurst number seven.

Jones points out that the position of the tee box is just as important as distance adjustment. When incorporating forward tees into a design on a dog leg, for instance, he takes a great deal of care in the placement of that tee. As he points out, "The dog leg may turn too quickly from the forward tee" so he's careful to place the tee so that "the player can hit a wood." He says, "Proper positioning is important to give the shorter hitter an opportunity to get closer to the green."

Additionally, he concerns himself with giving the player from the forward tee the appropriate variety of shots offered to golfers who play from other tees. Jones says, "When you add forward tees to a course you have to make sure that every par three isn't 99 yards long and each par four and five doesn't turn out to be the same length. This has become a problem with some redesigns. You should design from the forward tees to allow for different shots into every green. The set up should

Golf course architecture *continued*

have some long approach shots and some short ones, just as it is designed for from the other tees."

Rees says that women's golf is being helped by the fact that architects are returning to the "older, classic style design." As he says, "We're opening the entrances to greens and shaping ramps into the putting surfaces. At some of my newer designs, I'm letting golfers have the option of bouncing or flying the ball into the green." To enhance this feature, Jones uses an irrigation system which keeps "the approaches dry while still maintaining the proper moisture content on the green," thereby allowing the golfer to "bounce the ball in on the dry approaches or fly it on the green surface that has a little more moisture content."

Jan Beljan

Jan Beljan is a designer with the firm of Fazio Golf Course Designers. Among Fazio's more famous designs are The Champion at PGA National, site of the PGA Senior Championship, Wild Dunes in South Carolina and Barton Creek in Texas.

Jan lists distance as her firm's most important consideration from the forward tees. But she notes that total distance from all tees is "contingent upon the topography of the land and the environmental situation of the property. Anywhere there's a great deal of wetlands you're constrained as to where you can actually place a tee." Thus what may look like an architect trying to discourage women golfers with forced carries over a wet land area may be the only design that fits the demands of the US federal government

mandates relating to land usage.

Like that of most good architects, Fazio's design philosophy from the teeing ground is to give the golfer an idea of the route they should follow as indicated by the fairway. From there it's up to the golfer to decide the risks they are willing to take. Their design includes "safe routes" as indicated in her statement, "We don't like to have forced carries at all. We like to have 'bail out' areas, to give low-ball hitters an opportunity to roll the ball into the safe area, though it may mean that they have to play a longer hole to take the safer route."

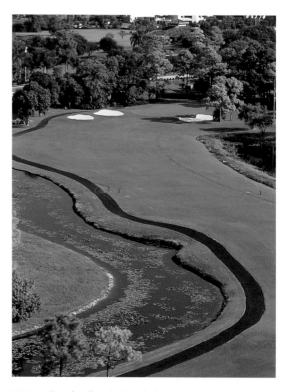

On the first hole of the Haig at PGA National, the fairway, the route from tee to green, shows how architect Tom Fazio intends the hole to be played, although a stronger player might cut some corners to shorten the distance.

Women's concerns

There is some concern about adding forward tees to older courses. Some women who have faced the challenges of minimal distance adjustment from the forward tees are, in some instances, reluctant to see "their course" redesigned. And architects are sensitive to the competitive nature and traditional sentiment of these women. Their comments offer an interesting insight to "the other side of the story" when it comes to adjusting yardage for the women.

Rees Jones

"Another problem with adding tees to older, shorter golf courses is that there is concern among some of the players that their course rating will change and it will affect their traveling handicaps in tournaments. If the course has an easier rating,

Modern architects must preserve wetlands so some forced carries are unavoidable.

the player's handicap index drops and the player must shoot a better score at other courses in order to compete."

Jan Beljan

"Women like a challenging golf course. In the north east, a lot of the forward tees were located in 1930, when a preponderance of men were playing, so you'll see total yardages from the forward tees of 5,600 to 5,900 yards. But for a golfer who hits the ball 130 yards, they wind up playing most holes with a driver and then a three wood. Even so there is some objection from women at older courses to changing this. In one instance I was called in by the golf pro and the greens committee to design forward tees with more significant

Women's concerns *continued*

yardage adjustment. They felt from the current distance the women weren't getting a fair shake. So I was asked, being also one of the distaff. But when I polled the women, the majority of whom had high handicaps, they didn't want the changes, and they didn't want their golf course taken from them. They also didn't want their course shortened because they knew their handicaps would drop and they wouldn't be able to compete in area invitationals. I never did redesign that course."

Alice Dye

"I've always been an advocate of two sets of tees for women, for all ranges of women amateurs, but so far that idea hasn't caught on. The forward yardage has been very successful. Most old clubs have done it or are considering it. I think the women have been down to the sun belt where there's almost always forward tees or they've been to England or Scotland where there's roll. And they think 'I can play these holes but when I go back to my old club I can't play it' so the women themselves have become more accepting of having a manageable golf course. With a 25 handicap, golf's a challenge anyway."

Most women-friendly course

In a 1995 *Golf for Women Magazine* survey, LPGA International Golf Course in Daytona Beach, Florida, won top honors for being the most "women friendly" golf course in the United States. Architect Rees Jones designed the layout and made history in the process. LPGA International Golf Course, site of the LPGA Tour's Sprint Titleholders Tournament, is the first course in history specifically designed to test the skills of the best female golfers in the world.

At another historic venue, The Country Club in Brookline, Massachusetts, Jones did major restoration work to the course before the 1988 Men's US Open and later some redesign of the forward tees in preparation for their hosting of the 1995 US Women's Amateur. After consultation with Judy Bell, head of the USGA championship committee, and club officials his challenge was to create appropriate forward tee locations for the tournament. Jones says, "Major attention was paid to the tee on the eighteenth hole because of the forced carry to the green. Our goal was to ensure it remained a demanding finishing hole, but not have it so long that longer hitters would have an unfair advantage so we added a new forward tee." Along with the forced carry Jones notes that the green is also one of the few at Brookline that is elevated and bunkered in front and their objective in redesign was to "make sure that every player who made it to the eighteenth hole wouldn't have an inordinately difficult second shot. By the same token we wanted it to be a challenging hole for the finish of a match." In doing so, Jones and the committee ensured that, if the final match consisted of a finesse player versus a power player, each would have a chance to win on the last hole.

Architect Rees Jones designed the LPGA International Golf Course, which was nominated the most "women-friendly" course in the United States.

How water changed the game

Architect and Amateur Champion Alice Dye remembers how well women could play longer courses before the fairways were irrigated. "Women used to be able to handle distance better because the fairways were firm. And before the mid-1950s we didn't have watered fairways at most golf courses." This effectively made the holes much shorter because the ball rolled 40 or 50 yards, and an emphasis was placed on accuracy rather than distance. Dye points out that, in a sense, women actually had an advantage over the men: "The men would hit these hard fairways, and if they were hooking the ball, the ball would roll 40 yards but end up in the trees."

With the advent of watered fairways, roll has been drastically reduced, so the long, less accurate hitter has the benefit of the ball stopping before it rolls off into trouble. The result, from Dye's observation, is that long golf courses that were once manageable for women have changed because of the loss of roll. She recalls that "senior players and women could play just fine until they started watering the fairways and after that it was over." The old saying, "short and straight" has lost its luster. From the perspective of Alice Dye's years of fine play and design she asserts that "the game has changed tremendously because golf used to be played on the ground; it's now played in the air." Hence her belief that the greatest consideration for a modern architect is to adjust the distance from the forward tees.

Fairness and the essence of the game

"The point of adjusting the tees is to give the player with less distance, but equal skill, the same club into the green as the longer hitter," says Jan Beljan of Fazio Design. This fairness is part of the essence of the game. She also stresses that the teachers of golf ought to explain to beginners, both men and women, that golf is about playing against the golf course, and its par. Jan says, "When you understand the concept of par, then you understand the game of golf."

Beljan adds meaning to this concept: "Another way of looking at it is a story I heard from Alice Dye about TPC Sawgrass. She said the men always want to play from the back tees, 'like the pro's play it.' But since the course is too long for them they come to a par five, and hit a driver, three wood, three wood and then a five iron to the green just like the average women's game when they have to play from yardages that are too long. The men think they've played it 'like the pros' but when was the last time you saw a pro hit a driver, three wood, three wood to a par five, never mind the five iron. It makes good sense that the yardages need to be adjusted." If the men were forced to play like this at their home course, either they'd quit or they'd make sure the course was redesigned with them in mind.

Beljan suggests that analogies like this make clear the importance of choosing the correct tees. She says, "When you play from tees that are too long you're selling yourself short because you won't be able to hit the proper club into the greens. Most greens are not designed to accept three woods. Some are designed to accept a nine iron or a seven iron, and, if you're not hitting that club, you can't expect to hold the green, first because the trajectory is much lower with a longer club and second because your hitting from so far away. Then you can fully expect to be hitting another shot back to the green with your wedge."

Jan Beljan of Fazio Design believes in adjusting tees to give players with less distance the same club into the green as long hitters.

Chapter twelve

Fitness

The following pages contain exercises that are recommended for golf fitness, but before starting any of these exercises you should consult with your physician and, if possible, begin your program with a qualified fitness trainer.

One reason for golf's popularity is the ability of almost anyone to enjoy it, regardless of age or fitness level. Athletes who played more strenuous sports, such as softball and tennis, often migrate to golf as they get older since it is less taxing on their bodies. Although it is true that a high fitness level isn't necessary for an enjoyable round of golf, there are common misconceptions that golf is free from the risk of injury, and that fitness and strength don't enhance performance very much.

A golf swing requires participation from almost every muscle in your body and can be particularly stressful to your back and shoulder muscles. A total body stretching routine, with special attention to the back and shoulders, should precede your practice sessions and every round of golf you play. And if you're serious about improving, whether you are a 36 handicap trying to knock 10 strokes off your game or an aspiring LPGA Tour player, a relevant fitness program should be part of your plan to achieve your goals.

To guide you through this process, we've chosen Randy Myers, Fitness Director at PGA National Resort and Spa and our golf school fitness consultant. Randy is one of the very few experts in golf-specific fitness training and he has worked with some of the top names in golf, including LPGA Tour star Michelle McGann.

His field of expertise is almost brand new. Ten years ago, professional golfers were just starting to get interested in the game-enhancing benefits of fitness and strength. Twenty-five years ago Gary Player, who also works with Myers, was almost alone in his dedication to golf fitness. In those days, golfers were skeptical of weight training because of the misconception that work-outs would render them muscle bound and inflexible, ruining their golf swings.

Today, if you took a sample of the top 50 money winners on each of the three major tours, LPGA, Senior, and PGA, you would find an overwhelming majority work out. Women especially have found the key to gaining distance is a combination of swing technique and muscular strength.

Myers' optimum golf fitness program for women focuses on four specific areas:

- Cardiovascular conditioning.
- Flexibility.
- Muscular endurance.
- Muscular strength.

Cardiovascular conditioning

If the final few holes of your golf round are characterized by errant shots and poor concentration, Myers suggests that your heart and lungs are not in good enough condition. Golf itself used to provide a good form of aerobic exercise, but with the prevalence of the golf cart, golfers need to supplement their aerobic work-outs. Myers suggests 30 minutes of sustained cardiovascular exercise, three times a week.

Since women are generally more flexible than men, improving and maintaining flexibility is an easy addition to your fitness routine. According to Myers, women who are free of injuries and have a fundamentally decent golf swing can improve their golf game almost immediately with a stretching program of just five to ten minutes a day. Golf-specific stretching should focus on the following areas: your legs, your middle and upper back, and the back of your shoulders.

The figure four stretch

1 To stretch your legs, buttocks and lower back, lie flat on your back with your knees bent at a right angle with your feet against a wall. Cross

your right leg over your left knee. Push down gently on your right knee and pull lightly on your right toes. Hold this position for 10 seconds and repeat three times for each leg.

Lower back rotation

2 To stretch your lower back, hips and shoulders, lie flat on your back with your hands behind your head. Cross your right foot over your left knee and slowly lower your right knee to the right. Let your lower torso follow but keep your

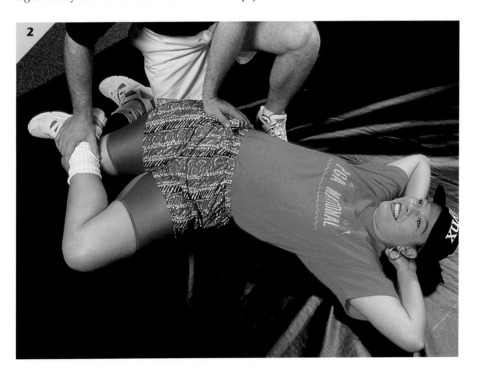

3

shoulders against the floor. Hold this position for 10 seconds and repeat three times for each leg.

Standing traction

3   For this exercise you need to stand near a doorway and place your left arm across your

hips and your right hand behind your head. Now move into the doorway so that your right elbow is against the side of the door jam. Slowly press your chest forward so that you build resistance in your right shoulder. Hold this position for 10 seconds and then repeat three times for each arm.

Stretching before you play

If you rush from your office to the first tee and don't have time to hit balls, at least take a few minutes to stretch the most injury-prone muscles used in your golf swing. Myers recommends "Stretches à la Cart," a simple pre-round routine for loosening up and avoiding injury.

Lower back/ hamstring stretch

1   To stretch your lower back and the back of your thighs, stand about a foot from the side of your golf cart and hold on to the handle

by the seat. Slowly stretch your body away from the cart until your arms are fully extended. Bend your knees slightly, then extend one heel out in front of you. Hold this position for 10 seconds and then repeat the exercise with your other leg.

1

Hip flexor lunges

2 To stretch your hips, rest a golf club shaft across your upper back and stand about two to three feet from the side of your golf cart. Keeping your left foot in the same location, stride forward with your right leg and plant your right foot onto the floor of the cart. Slowly shift your weight over your right leg but be sure your right knee does not extend past your right toes. Also, be sure to adjust your distance from the cart based on the length of your legs and your flexibility. Repeat this stretch 3 times with each leg.

Shoulder stretch

3 You can stretch your shoulders by extending your arm at shoulder height and grasping one of the rails that supports the roof of your cart. Slowly turn your upper body away from your extended arm until you feel some tension in your shoulder. Repeat this stretch 3 times with each arm.

147

Building muscular strength

The next two areas of concern are muscular endurance and strength in which, from Myers' experience, many women golfers are severely deficient. A qualified fitness trainer should test your leg strength, upper body strength and muscular endurance, and then outline a program for strengthening these areas. Myers warns that if you don't have the option of being tested in these areas, it is especially important to start your program slowly, as a majority of injuries occur within the first two weeks of beginning an exercise regimen.

Benefits of muscular strength

Although it is a great asset, muscular strength by itself doesn't produce distance in golf. Club head speed and solidness of contact are necessary to produce maximum distance, but if you lose your grip on the club or you can't hold your body steady in certain positions during your swing, you'll never hit the ball properly.

Hands, wrists and arms

The first crucial strength area is your hands since they are your only connection to the club. Your hands are supported by the muscles of your wrists and arms and it is vital that these muscles are strong for club control. How strong should you be? Strong enough to grip the club lightly and still maintain complete control over it. Of the thousands of women we teach, an extremely high percentage of them lose control of the golf club near the top of the swing. This is especially disturbing when the rest of their swing motion is good, and their mis-hits are simply a result of not being strong enough to control the weight of the club at the top of their swing. As Myers explains,

a majority of women golfers have difficulty maintaining their hold on the club because of weak wrist and forearm muscles.

Leg strength

The legs provide overall stability for the complete motion of your golf swing and help maintain the posture you establish at address. Although women often have strong muscles in the front of their thighs, their inner and outer thigh muscles are often weak as are the largest mid-body muscles, the gluteal complex that make up your rear end. When these muscles are weak they cannot be used as a platform to support your golf swing.

Shoulder strength

Another area Myers stresses is shoulder strength, which he sees as a key to keeping correct posture during your swing and good alignment at address. His program includes development of your front and rear shoulder muscles because they are not used as much in everyday life. Since your triceps muscles make up two-thirds of your upper arm, they are very involved in your golf swing, especially as your arms extend through impact.

Myers' program helps keep both triceps equally developed and strong.

Women are often injured when they try to hit down on the ball and instead hit the ground behind the ball. This jarring impact can cause trauma to the elbow and shoulder muscles so it's a good idea for the muscles surrounding these joints to be strong. Along with perfecting their swing, women should also develop strong lower and upper arm muscles to help avoid injuries associated with hitting into the ground.

Some simple strength-training exercises

Although we strongly recommend you begin your program with a fitness trainer, you can do the following exercises at home as an alternative. If you've never done strength training before you may want to start these exercises in the first few days without using any weights at all. Then gradually add weights in small increments, say, two-pound dumb bells. If you don't have dumb bells, try substituting a can of soup in each hand or plastic bottles of soda. It is beneficial to put your muscles through the full range of motion using the required repetitions. The best approach is to start slowly and add weight gradually to guard against the possibility of injury.

Seated forearm curls

1 To strengthen your wrists and forearms, sit in a chair and rest the back of your forearm against your thigh with your wrist extended beyond your knee. With your palm facing up, slowly lower and raise your wrist by flexing and extending your wrist and keeping your forearm in place. Do 10 repetitions and then switch arms. Then repeat the sequence with your palm starting in a face-down position.

Wall side shoulder raise

To strengthen your mid shoulders and forearms, start from a standing position with your back against a wall and your feet shoulder width apart. Bend your knees into a semi-squatting position and let your arms hang at your sides. Slowly raise your arms vertically until they are at shoulder height, then lower them slowly back to your sides. Repeat 10 times.

Wall front shoulder raise

2 To strengthen the front of your shoulder, set up as you did for the "wall side shoulder raise" and position your hands in front of your thighs. Slowly raise your hands to eye level and lower them slowly back to your thighs. Repeat 10 times.

Bent over rear shoulder raise

To strengthen the back of your shoulders and your upper back, bend from your waist and support your head in your left arm or against a wall. Let your right arm hang straight down to the ground. Slowly raise

Building muscular strength *continued*

your arm straight out to the side until it's at shoulder height. Lower your arm slowly back to your side. Repeat 10 times, then repeat with your left arm.

Flat chest press

3 To strengthen your chest and shoulders, lie on your back and hold a weight in each hand. Slowly lift your arms until they are directly over your head and then move your hands in to meet each other over your head. Lower your arms slowly back to the ground. Repeat 10 times.

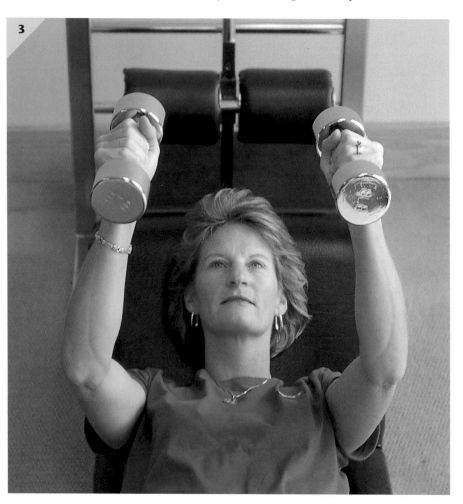

Two arm triceps extensions

To strengthen the triceps in the back of your upper arm, lie on your back and hold a weight in each hand. Bend your elbows until they point to the ceiling and your hands are adjacent to your ears. Slowly raise and lower the weights by bending your elbows while your upper arms remain stationary. Repeat 12 times.

Single hip raises

4 To strengthen your outer thighs and buttocks, lie on your left side and hold a weight on your right hip. Slowly raise your leg up and down, being sure to limit the motion to your hips to isolate the hip muscles. Repeat 10 times for each leg.

Calf raises

5 To strengthen your calves and Achilles tendons, start this exercise by standing about one foot away from a wall with your arms against the wall. Then lean your body weight forward as you stand up on your toes. Make sure that you extend up as high as you can to achieve maximum stretching of your calves. This exercise can easily be enhanced by working one leg at a time. To do so, loop your right foot behind your left and slowly raise your left leg as above. Repeat the motion 10 times and then switch legs.

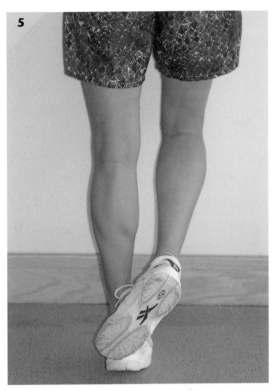

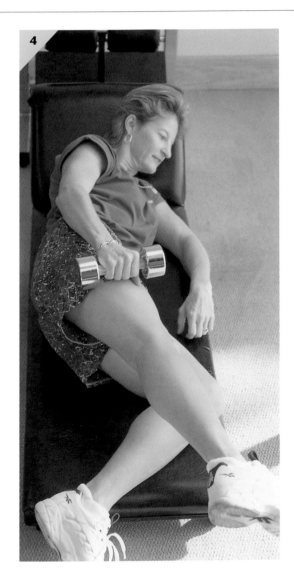

Alternating lunges

6 To strengthen the back and front of your thighs, hold a weight in each hand and take a normal stride with one leg while the other remains stationary. Then slowly bend both knees until your back knee touches the ground. Do not allow your front knee to extend out over your front toe. Alternate the motion with each leg until you've done it 10 times per leg.

Your first year as a golfer

From the outside, golf seems like a simple game but your first few rounds can prove an arduous task. The golf course offers a variety of situations, each requiring a different club, and sometimes a modified swing and set up. There are rules to learn, customs to follow, and a pace of play to be maintained. All combine to create a good bit of confusion for the beginner. And

though this book will clarify some of your confusion, you'll need time to master your skills, learn golf's nuances, and make yourself at home on the course.

For this reason, we offer modifications you can make during your first year as a golfer. Keep in mind, our suggestions are not in accordance with the official Rules of Golf, and are by no means suggested for play when your swing matures. But when you're just learning golf, it's almost impossible to know all the rules, let alone follow them and still complete 18 holes in four hours. Golf is a complex game and, just like anything else you learn, you need to start simple and work toward the more difficult. If you begin your golf career trying to play in strict accordance to the Rules it's akin to learning algebra before you learn addition.

Once you're more comfortable on the golf course, begin to familiarize yourself with the Rules of Golf. They are the essence of the game and a true round of golf can only be played when you follow the rules to the letter.

Your first few rounds

If possible, arrange to play your first few rounds with an experienced player. Don't worry that you won't play as well as they do—you're a beginner and therefore you have a perfect excuse. Another choice is to schedule a playing lesson with your golf professional. In both cases, you'll have someone to answer your questions and show you around the course.

Chapter thirteen

Dog leg

Refers to the shape of some golf holes, so named for their resemblance to a dog's hind leg. These holes bend from left to right or right to left.

Dormie

In matchplay you are said to be "dormie" when you lead by the same number of holes that are left to be played. You'll be dormie when you're three up with three holes to play.

Driver

The object off a par four and five is to hit or drive your ball down the fairway. The club of choice is often a one wood, most commonly referred to as a driver. It should hit the ball the furthest of all the clubs in your bag.

Drop zone

Drop zones are marked areas on the course where you can take relief from certain situations, such as ground under repair, wet areas, or temporary immovable obstructions. On some courses, where there are long, forced carries, drop areas are available, at your option, when your shot doesn't clear the water hazard. Often they are located closer to the hole so that the length of the carry is diminished.

A group of beginners

If you decide to play your first round with other new golfers be sure each of you makes some advance preparations. First, make a tee time (an appointment to play) when the course is less crowded so you can take a little more time than more experienced players need. Next, be sure to watch a few rounds of golf on TV. Though your shots probably won't look like those of the pros, observe how they move around the course and the conditions of play subject to commentary. Most importantly, be sure you have taken a lesson or spent some productive time on the practice range before you venture onto the course.

The first tee

This can be a nerve-wracking place even for more experienced players. It's often in view of the clubhouse so you'll feel like a lot of "eyes" are on you. The common reaction is to rush, but slow down, evaluate your target, and go through your preshot routine. This way you'll increase your odds of getting off to a good start. If you badly mis-hit your first shot, a common practice is to take one "mulligan" (another try). Since "mulligans" are not in accordance with the rules, you'd only do so in a casual round if time allows.

Improving your lie

Especially during your first few rounds move your ball from difficult lies (heavy rough, bare ground, difficult stances) onto good ones. If someone tells you you're breaking the rules, explain that you're

Especially during your first few rounds, move your ball off difficult lies like this one and play from a good lie.

trying to learn the easier shots before you tackle the more difficult ones and you're not playing for an official score. There is little sense in trying to hit a ball from heavy rough when you're still challenged by a shot from a good lie in the fairway.

Moving along

If you hit a ball that travels only a few yards from the tee, pick it up, bring it out to the fairway where the other members of your group have hit their shots, and play from there. During your first few rounds you may find that several shots in a row go badly. Instead of worrying about holding up the others, just pick up your ball, collect your thoughts, and take another turn after the other members of your group have hit.

153

playing extremely slowly."

Handicap

Though tournament handicaps are computed with a complicated formula, for a general guide your handicap is the number of strokes your average score is over par.

Hazard

This term is strictly defined in the Rules of Golf, but, generally speaking, it is an obstacle of water or sand on a golf course.

Heavy

See *Fat*.

Hold the green

A shot that stays on the green is said to have held the green. "I hit that ball too low and it couldn't hold the green."

Hole

The goal of golf is to get your ball in the hole in as few shots as possible; it's also referred to as the cup.

Hole in one

When you hit your ball from the tee and it goes in the hole you've made a hole in one. Although a rarity, it usually happens on a par three.

Inside the leather

In golf lingo, a ball that comes to rest within an area no greater than the length of your putter's grip is said to be inside the leather (of your grip). Casually

speaking, these putts are said to be "gimmies" (see *Gimmie*).

Irons

The irons, which refer to the material they are most often made from, produce progressively more height and less length, e.g. a nine iron goes much higher and shorter than a four iron. Used for the accuracy required to hit and "hold" greens.

Jail

When your ball comes to rest behind a stand of trees or other blockades, then you have put yourself in jail.

Jumper lie

In the rough, when the grass grows in the direction you intend to hit your ball, the ball "jumps" off the club face and travels a greater distance than normal.

Landing area

The ideal spot to land your ball in the fairway.

Lie angle

The angle the shaft creates with the ground as measured from the mid point of the shaft.

Lift, clean, and place

Under certain conditions, The Rules of Golf and/or local rules allow you to lift, clean, and place your ball back on the grass. Normally, the ball is played as it

lies and you are prohibited from touching it until it comes to rest on the green, but if the course is extremely wet, this rule may be put into effect.

Local rules

In addition to the Rules of Golf, sometimes there are additional rules based on idiosyncrasies of their course.

Loft

The angle your club face forms with the ground, i.e. how much the face of your club looks at the sky.

Match

Matchplay is where you play against a competitor and either win, lose or tie (known as halve) each hole played until the match is decided. For every hole you win, you are "one up" and for every hole you lose you are "one down." When you win the match on the seventeenth hole, it's called "two and one", i.e. you're two up with only one hole to play. If you lost the match on the twelfth hole, you've lost seven and six—seven down with six holes to play.

Medal

In medal competitions the lowest score wins and the winner is deemed the "medalist." This form of play is also commonly

known as stroke play.

Metal wood

Woods were originally so named because their heads were crafted from wood. Now they are more often made of metal or other materials, and are referred to as "metal woods."

Par

The number of shots required by an expert to complete a hole. The total of all the pars gives the "course par," e.g. "it's a par 72" layout.

Pin

See *Flagstick*.

Pitch

A lofted shot played from an area around the green (compare to *Chip*).

Play it as it lies

Under the Rules of Golf, you are obliged to play the ball as it has come to rest on the course (compare to *Lift, clean, and place*).

Play through

If the group of golfers ahead of you is playing too slowly they may ask you to "play through" which means they will stand aside and let you play the hole, then resume play. The pace of play at most courses is designed for foursomes so if the course is crowded and you're playing in a twosome or onesome (by yourself) don't expect to be asked to play through.

Preferred lies

Also known as "winter rules," preferred lies indicate that you can roll the ball onto a better lie in the fairway. This is against the Rules of Golf but is often used in casual competition when the condition of the fairways is poor. If you answer "yes" to the question "Are we rolling them today?" you're playing preferred lies.

Release

During the backswing an important angle of power is created between the left arm and the club shaft. Once this 90-degree angle is made it must be released just before impact so that the club and ball meet with solid contact. If you hold this angle for too long or let it go too early, you've ruined your release and you won't hit the ball as far as you should.

Recovery shot

If you hit your shot into trouble and get yourself out of this bad situation you are said to have hit a nice "recovery shot."

Royal & Ancient Golf Club of St. Andrews

This organization, in conjunction with the United States Golf Association, has established

The Rules of Golf. It is casually referred to as the "R & A."

Rub of the green

When your ball takes an unfair bounce it's known as the run of the green or, more commonly, as a bad luck.

Sand save

When your approach shot misses the green and lands in a bunker, you'll make what's known as "sand save" when you hit your ball from the bunker onto the green and sink the putt for a par. Also known as a "sandie" or a good "up and down."

Shaft flex

During the swing, the shaft of a properly fit club flexes from side to side and bows downward. This is intensified during the downswing where the shaft kicks into the ball at impact. Shafts come in various flexes. Too stiff a shaft causes a loss of distance and a low trajectory. You should swing the most flexible shaft you can handle.

Side wind

See *Cross wind*.

Sky ball

See *Pop up*.

Snowman

When you make a score of eight on a hole it's known as a "snowman" due to the number's

resemblance to a snowman.

Starter

Before you begin your round of golf, many courses have you check in with an employee known as the starter. This person makes sure you have paid the appropriate fees, advises you of local rules and makes sure you tee off at the proper time.

Static fit

Trying to fit clubs without the client hitting golf balls.

Stroke

1 An upper body motion used for putting and chipping.

2 The point system in golf: each time you hit a ball it counts as a stroke. Your total number of strokes is your score.

Stroke play

See *Medal*.

Sweet spot

The ideal contact point on the face of every club: woods, iron and putter. The sweet spot is the perfectly balanced center of the club face which produces the most solid contact with minimal turning or twisting at impact.

Target line

An imaginary line extending from your ball to your target.

Tee shot

The shot you hit from the teeing ground of any golf hole.

Tee time

A reservation for a round of golf.

Thin

When the leading edge makes contact too high on the back edge of the golf ball you've hit what's known as a "thin shot" (compare to *Fat*).

Trajectory

Depending on what club you choose, a well-hit golf shot travels on different trajectories because of the loft of each club. Trajectory is the up and down curve of your golf ball.

Trap

Slang term for a sand bunker. You won't find the word "trap" in the rule book; it's a bunker, either sand or grass.

USGA

The United States Golf Association, in conjunction with the Royal & Ancient Golf Club of St. Andrews, has established The Rules of Golf. Casually referred to as the "USGA."

Whippy

A shaft that is too flexible for the golfer swinging it. A whippy shaft bows and bends excessively during the swing and causes a wild shot pattern—some left, some right, and some hooks mixed with slices.

Winter rules

See *Preferred lies*.